FREE THE COPTS

From Ancient Glory to Modern Oppression

~

THE AUSTRALIAN COPTIC MOVEMENT ASSOCIATION

~Edited by Ramy Tadros~

FREE THE COPTS

The Australian Coptic Movement Association

~

The Australian Coptic Movement Association Ltd

PO Box 30 | St Clair| NSW 2759 | Australia

www.auscma.com| info@auscma.com

~

ISBN-13: 978-0-9875966-0-4

CONTENTS

ABOUT THE AUSTRALIAN COPTIC MOVEMENT

The Australian Coptic Movement Association Ltd (ACM) was founded in 2010 by experienced Coptic rights activists and a new generation of passionate young Copts and non-Copts from across Australia. The ACM is a community advocacy group that fights for human rights in Egypt by exposing the persecution suffered by Copts, advocating for greater political and civil liberties, and calling for the justice and security of Copts in order to promote democratic change.

By closely working with the wider Australian community, government bodies, the media, and other human rights organisations, ACM has quickly grown to become one of the most active Coptic organisations in Australia, accumulating nationwide support. This status is reflected and recorded in Hansard records and numerous national and international media reports.

The ACM has achieved many milestones, which has brought it to the forefront of the struggle for freedom. These achievements include organising rallies, lobbying the Australian government to pass motions in the Federal and NSW Houses of Parliament, conducting letter-writing campaigns, releasing media statements, providing support to Coptic asylum seekers, and encouraging Copts to assimilate into the wider community.

To support the ACM's cause, please visit the following website: <http://www.auscma.com>.

PREFACE

Peter Tadros

In Chapter Two of this book, senior journalist and author Peter Day writes,

Sadly, the situation does not seem much better in the Middle Eastern studies departments of many Western universities. This is of particular significance, because Western correspondents writing about foreign affairs for the major media are usually graduates of those universities. That is to say, they have been trained in the heartland of political correctness, where it continues to be enforced with ever-greater ferocity. As a consequence, intellectual timidity and careerism reign supreme.

Day, like all the contributors to *Free the Copts*, presents in-depth knowledge about Egypt, the region, and, of course, the Copts. Day's analysis of the Muslim Brotherhood, their history, and their relationships with previous Egyptian regimes is remarkable.

The recent upheaval in the Middle East and North Africa, which is now spreading to other parts of Africa, has taken the focus away from the plight of Egypt's Copts and other minorities in the region. At the time of writing, there is no end in sight to the conflict in Syria, and UN estimates suggest that up to 60,000 people might have been killed as of 13 February 2013. Fierce debates are raging as to whether or not Western countries should be supporting the rebels as they try to topple the Assad Regime. Syrian Christians also face an unknown future, and like the Copts in Egypt they are among the most vulnerable groups in

Syria, jammed between the Asaad Regime on one side and the rebels on the other.

Libya is also a flashpoint, and Copts who live in Libya have come under attacks, with many detained, tortured, and killed. The so-called Arab Spring—the revolutions that swept Tunisia, Egypt, Libya, and other Middle Eastern countries—has shifted direction from being a fight for freedom to a struggle against Islamic extremism. Meanwhile, the region's Christian minorities are being driven out of their homes and nations.

This excerpt, from a *New York Times* report dated 13 February 2013, shows the suffering that Syria's Christians are facing:

> The bright voices of children at play echoed off the ancient walls of Mor Hanonyo last week, breaking centuries of stillness in this 1,600-year-old Syriac Orthodox monastery outside Mardin in southeastern Turkey. Little boys skipped around the monastery courtyard zipped up in quilted winter jackets, while their elders huddled indoors and lamented the violence and mayhem that have forced them to flee their homes in Syria.
>
> One mother told of the abduction of a neighbor's child, held for ransom by rebel fighters in her hometown of Al-Hasakah, which prompted her family to seek safety for their three young sons across the border in Turkey. A young man demonstrated how he was hung by his arms, robbed and beaten by rebels, "just for being a Christian".
>
> Violence against Christians is escalating in the governorate of Al-Hasakah in north-eastern Syria, which is home to tens of thousands of Syriac Christians, the refugees said.
>
> The region, known locally as the Jazeera, encompasses the districts of Ras al-Ain, Qamishli and Malikiyah. With government forces, Arab rebels of the Free Syrian Army and Kurdish fighters locked in a three-way struggle for control, the area's Christian population has found itself caught in the middle.
>
> While fighting is sporadic, the region has succumbed to lawlessness, and Christians have become the target of armed rebel gangs, Father Gabriel Akyuz, the metropolitan vicar of Mardin, said in an interview in Mardin last week.
>
> "The gangs are kidnapping people and holding them to ransom. They are perpetrating great injustices. That is why Syriacs are fleeing," he said.[1]

The news item written by Susanne Gusten ends in a statement from a 36-year-old pathologist who says, "As Christians in the Middle East,

---

[1] For more information, see <http://www.nytimes.com/2013/02/14/world/middleeast/christians-squeezed-out-by-violent-struggle-in-north-syria.html?pagewanted=all&_r=0>. This article was accessed on 1 June 2013.

we live in misery and suffer many difficulties. We want nothing more than to emigrate to other places."

At the time of writing, we also learned of the kidnapping of two orthodox bishops in Syria. Yet just weeks prior to this incident, one of the largest cathedrals in the Middle East and North Africa (MENA) region came under attack for the first time. Egyptians and, in particular, Coptic Christians watched in shock as a funeral service at Saint Mark's Coptic Orthodox Cathedral in Cairo came under attack by armed thugs and Egyptian police. Those attacked were gathering to attend a mass funeral service for Copts who were massacred in the district of Khosous, just north of Cairo. This is part of the statement issued on 12 April 2013 by His Grace Bishop Anba Suriel, the bishop of the Coptic Orthodox Diocese of Melbourne and Affiliated Regions:

> St Mark's Cathedral in Abbassiya, Cairo, is the International Headquarters of the Coptic Orthodox Church. Hence it holds a great symbolic significance in the hearts of all Copts worldwide. A red line has been crossed by Muslim mobs that attacked Copts at a very vulnerable moment. This incident makes you wonder what type of human beings would attack people when they are mourning the killing of their loved ones?
>
> These Copts were killed simply for being Christians and not only killed but one was burnt alive! I cannot fathom nor comprehend the lack of sympathy by such Muslim mobs when seeing fellow humans going to bury their dead, they use the opportunity to show hatred and contempt towards the Copts.[2]

It is suggested that the environment you grow up in is partly responsible for shaping your views on life; however, sometimes a one-off event or experience can also influence the way you view the world. I always get asked, "Why are you so concerned? What makes you so interested in Egypt's Copts? You are Australian born and do not know much about the reality on the ground in Egypt. Focus on your education and work." It is as if those Copts who are born outside of Egypt should not be concerned with the welfare of their country of origin or the plight of their people back home. One should, instead, just enjoy the new-found freedoms of the foreign land they were lucky enough to born into. The majority seem to take this path, and the same might be said about other immigrant communities in the West. Other passive voices prefer not to get involved, citing Christian religious

---

[2] See <http://www.copticworld.org/articles/1928/>. This webpage was accessed on 1 June 2013.

teaching in their defence. They use their skewed interpretation of selective biblical verses to silence others. And, then, there are those who use the "adverse effect" argument as an excuse to do nothing, fearing that, by taking action here, it will bring about more calamity on those living in Egypt. A few see human rights advocacy as a form of politics, and use this argument to be inactive and continue with their daily routine. Thankfully, though, we are seeing a new generation of Coptic rights activists—in Egypt and abroad—and clergy who continue to speak out and defend the rights of the oppressed. Copts are not alone, as we see from the many articles in this book by non-Coptic contributors who have kindly volunteered their time.

One particular incident that increased the interest in the Coptic rights movement was the consecutive attacks against Copts in the village of el-Kosheh near Luxor in Upper Egypt. In 1998, I recall receiving a letter titled "A cry for help from Egypt". The letter originated from the village of el-Kosheh and was notifying us of a terrible incident, where more than 1,000 Coptic Christians were being tortured en masse by the Egyptian security forces to coerce them into falsely admitting that a fellow Copt was responsible for killing Copts and Muslims from the same village. We were listening to Nadia Ghaly's Egyptian radio programme in Melbourne, when full details of the torture were exposed by the brave Bishop of the Baliana diocese in the province of Sohag. His Eminence Bishop Wissa publicised the atrocities that were taking place in el-Kosheh, while acknowledging that his phone was being tapped by the Egyptian Government.

I was inspired by this brave bishop who went to extreme lengths to share his pain with the rest of the world, at a time when few spoke out about such issues in Egypt. We then commenced several protests and attempted to create awareness to spread the cry from the streets of Egypt to the streets of Australia. The torture ceased—but the injustices continued. And a Copt known as Shaiboob William was sentenced to 15 years of hard labour for a crime he did not commit. During those three years, we organised many events and rallies in the middle of Sydney City. I remember on 1 January 2000 organising a mock funeral where we carried 21 coffins representing the 21 Copts who were massacred in el-Kosheh. The replica coffins looked so real that some onlookers stood still paying their respects. A few weeks later there was an unrelated protest in Sydney, and we noticed they copied our idea and carried replica coffins in their protest march. Many of the younger members and supporters of the Australian Coptic Movement

Association (ACM) were present at these protests more than a decade ago, and they remember these events as young children.

From 2001 to February 2010, I was working in the field as an individual. After this solo period, a group of energetic men and women from various backgrounds gathered together and founded the ACM. The group included middle-aged individuals, who had a history of Coptic rights advocacy, and a new breed of activists in their twenties and thirties. These individuals sought to take action and to bring justice to the families of all victims in Egypt. And this mobilisation occurred following the 2010 Christmas Eve massacre in the city of Naga Hamadi, where six young Coptic Christians were gunned down outside a Church. The incident sparked grief and anger from the Coptic community in Egypt and all over the world.

In a short period of time, this group was able to spread its message to thousands of people in the wider community and grab the attention of many Australian politicians, from councillors at the local council to senior cabinet ministers at the federal parliament.

It was 9 October 2011, and an unprecedented event had just occurred in Egypt. I recall checking my social media accounts and seeing a sea of blood on my Facebook wall as images filtered through of a terrible massacre. Our organisation was inundated with enquiries and suggestions about a proposed response following the brutal *Maspero Massacre* in downtown Cairo, which claimed dozens of lives and left more than 200 injured. The few hours of terror were captured by private media outlets and amateur video. The heinous attack against Coptic protestors made international headlines for several days, as the Egyptian military—which was ultimately responsible for the attack— blamed unidentified "third parties".

The Maspero Massacre was the first time that the Egyptian military had attacked Coptic protestors with such force. Some commentators suggested that an enemy at war would not be treated with such brutality. The massacre was a devastating and demoralising event for all Coptic Christians. It was as if the military wanted to teach the Copts a lesson and to get them off the streets. On 10 October 2011, Nina Shea, the director for the Centre of Religious Freedom, described the Maspero Massacre as follows:

> The real significance of this is that it signals the future treatment of the Christian Coptic community by the state. The military was their last hope in protecting them from lawless forces in society that were religiously motivated to [eradicate]

them, namely the Salafis. Now they know they have no protection.

I think we can expect to see a major exodus of Coptic Christians from Egypt. This is a watershed moment. The whole reason they were in the streets was to protest lawless forces. It extinguishes all hope for them. They are utterly vulnerable.

The US Administration responded to the massacre by calling for "restraint" from both sides, thus equating the Coptic protestors with the powerful (and partly US-backed) Egyptian military. This caused outrage among Copts and sympathisers alike. The ACM then proceeded to organise a mass rally on 23 October 2011, which was attended by thousands of Copts and many of the most senior members from the Australian Federal Government and the New South Wales State Government.

Amidst all the chaos, and as clashes were continuing following the Maspero Massacre, the ACM received an e-mail from an Australian named Ramy Christopher Tadros (unrelated to me). This is what the message said:

To the Australian Coptic Movement,

I would like to join the Australian Coptic Movement, and help in your campaigning activities for our brothers and sisters in Egypt. You may also find me useful, because I am a professional writer and editor.

I look forward to hearing from you soon.

With Tadros' assistance, we prepared a 1,000-word tribute to His Holiness Pope Shenouda III of Alexandria to honour the life of this great man. The tribute was released on 22 April 2012. We were delighted to learn that it was also included in a textbook for students learning writing skills at Sydney Community College. This will be read by thousands of Australian students every year for years to come. From here, the idea of publishing a book about Egypt's Copts was first discussed.

Initially, we were going to publish an e-book containing the tribute only. Then, we thought about publishing a short booklet summarising all of ACM's activities, including our media releases. The idea evolved further when we felt we were in need of a book discussing the plight of Egypt's Copts, including their culture and history. The project was quite ambitious in light of the minimal resources available to the ACM. All the members are volunteers.

Tadros made *Free the Copts* possible by sacrificing more than six months of his time to edit and format the book and to make it suitable for online distribution across the world. And we are indebted to him for this.

In the last few years, we have seen an increase in media coverage and awareness of the hardships of Egypt's Copts. However, for the second- or third-generation Copts born in the diaspora, there are few resources available that explain the Egyptian Copt's predicament. Although there are many books focusing on the history of the Coptic Orthodox Church and the great saints and martyrs, there are few publications that provide a more detailed snapshot of Egypt's Copts and their struggle against Islamisation and the rise of the Muslim Brotherhood. *Free the Copts* aims to close this gap. It is written to help enlighten all worldwide readers, whether they are Copts or not.

We hope this book is considered fairly and seriously by all peace-loving people of the world, and we hope you join us at the ACM in our quest for justice.

~~~~~~

Peter Tadros has participated in fact-finding missions and presented at many seminars. He features regularly in the media for commentary on Egypt and the plight of Copts, including regular radio interviews, print features, and television appearances. Tadros is one of the founding members of the Australian Coptic Movement Association.

PART I

~

POLITICS, THE PEOPLE, AND THE PRESENT

1. EDITOR'S INTRODUCTION:
UNDER SIEGE

Ramy Tadros

T hey struck the heart of the holy order. Bigoted mobs, local residents, state security forces—each reinforced the other as they attacked hundreds of Copts trapped inside Saint Mark's Coptic Orthodox Cathedral, Cairo, on Sunday 7 April 2013.[3]

The mobs pelted rocks, hurled broken bottles, and catapulted chunks of masonry at the confined Christians. The local residents lobbed Molotov cocktails and shot their guns at any Coptic man, woman, or child penned in the cathedral.[4] And the Egyptian State's security forces fired canister after canister of US-supplied and Obama-endorsed tear gas into the cathedral's compound.[5]

---

[3] See *The Independent*, "Coptic Christians under siege as mob attacks Cairo cathedral", 8 April 2013. This report was accessed on 18 May 2013 at <http://www.independent.co.uk/news/world/africa/coptic-christians-under-siege-as-mob-attacks-cairo-cathedral-8563600.html>.

[4] See the Gatestone Institute, "The Siege of Egypt's St Mark Cathedral: An Insider's Account", 22 April 2013. This article was accessed on 19 May 2013 at <http://www.gatestoneinstitute.org/3680/egypt-st-mark-cathedral>.

[5] See *The Commentator*, "US teargas arrives in Egypt for Muslim Brotherhood use", 9 April 2013. This article was accessed on 18 May 2013 at <http://www.thecommentator.com/article/3200/us_teargas_arrives_in_egypt_for_muslim_brotherhood_use>.

One bystander even recorded a video showing police officers helping local residents improve their aim; apparently, a few civilians had yet to master the sights on their new handguns.[6] And what better opportunity would emerge to enhance their shooting skills? An unarmed and cornered Coptic Christian congregation can neither fight nor take flight.

In the end, two Copts died and more than 89 were injured in the 12-hour siege of Saint Mark's Cathedral.

Yet just the day before this siege, a Muslim rabble murdered five Copts in Khosous, a town north of Cairo. And it was in response to these crimes at Khosous that the congregation had assembled for a mass funeral at Saint Mark's Cathedral in Cairo. So what began as a mass funeral to mourn the dead of Khosous turned into a fresh massacre. The Christian mourners themselves became the target of Islamist rage.

Although Egypt's Copts have endured worse tragedies, the siege of Saint Mark's Cathedral is symbolic. It represents a terrifying and unprecedented development in the war against every minority in the Middle East.

Nowhere is secure.

Nothing is sacred.

No one is safe.

I am slouching in an armchair 14,400 kilometres away from Saint Mark's Cathedral in Cairo. A caffè latte rests on the table in front of me. Laughter and chit-chat surround me, and the café is buzzing with movement. It is lunchtime in Sydney's central business district, and many office workers are darting around the place. Although a few have come for a quick meal, the majority are lined up for an espresso—a caffeine fix to help them through the sluggish afternoon.

Because of the modern world's wonders, I am reading about the siege of Saint Mark's Cathedral on my iPad. I flick through several articles and notice the politically correct—almost misleading—reporting that is spewing out of the major news outlets. The BBC, for

---

[6] See Fox News, "New video shows Egyptian police allowing deadly attack on Coptic cathedral", 28 April 2013. This article was accessed on 17 May 2013 at <http://www.foxnews.com/world/2013/04/28/new-video-shows-egyptian-police-allowing-attack-on-coptic-cathedral/>.

example, reports that "two people were killed in clashes outside Cairo's main cathedral on Sunday".[7] And later in the same article, it says,

Mourners leaving St Mark's Cathedral clashed with local residents. Police fired tear gas to break up the violence. More than 89 people were injured, the state news agency said.

Clashes and *clashed?* A clash suggests a fair fight between two equally matched forces. Is this the best word the BBC's journalist could find to describe a siege, an assault, an atrocity?

Or what about the BBC's lie, also in the same news report, that "Police fired tear gas to break up the violence"? Yes, police fired tear gas—but it was not to break up the violence. According to *The Independent*, and many other sources, police fired tear gas *at the Christians trapped inside the cathedral compound*:

The security forces positioned outside the cathedral launched volley after volley of tear gas into the compound [Saint Mark's Coptic Orthodox Cathedral in Cairo]. Some of the thousands of onlookers gathered in the road cheered as the canisters rocketed towards Christians ...[8]

So there it is: two different pictures of the same reality. The distorted and politically correct picture comes from the BBC, which is a major news outlet, whereas the more accurate picture emerges from *The Independent*, a smaller news outlet.[9]

---

[7] See the BBC, "Toll rises in Cairo clashes at Coptic Cathedral", 8 April 2013. This article was accessed on 17 May 2013 at <http://www.bbc.co.uk/news/world-middle-east-22062622>.

[8] See *The Independent*, "Coptic Christians under siege as mob attacks Cairo cathedral", 8 April 2013. This report was accessed on 18 May 2013 at <http://www.independent.co.uk/news/world/africa/coptic-christians-under-siege-as-mob-attacks-cairo-cathedral-8563600.html>.

[9] For more information about mainstream news outlets and their liberal bias, see Groseclose, T & Milyo, J 2005, "A Measure of Media Bias", *The Quarterly Journal of Economics*, vol. CXX, issue 4, pp. 1191–1237. You can download a copy of this research from <http://www.sscnet.ucla.edu/polisci/faculty/groseclose/pdfs/MediaBias.pdf>. This file was downloaded on 26 March 2013. Groseclose also published a book, *Left Turn: How the Liberal Media Bias Distorts the American Mind*, which expands on this research.

Today, however, this kind of politically correct reporting plagues all areas of liberal journalism. Take *Time* magazine, another major news outlet like the BBC. When *Time* places the Egyptian President Mohamed Morsi on its shortlist for the Person of the Year 2012 award, then I know the quality—maybe even honesty—of mainstream journalism has been levelled to junk status.[10]

But all these news reports, even the politically correct liberal revisions, are sobering. Life may be good here in Sydney, Australia, but on the other side of the planet a Christian minority is suffering at the hands of a Muslim majority. Coptic girls are being abducted every week. Churches are being routinely torched. And Christians are even being terrorised. The most recent terrorist bombing happened at the Saints Coptic Orthodox Church in Alexandria, during a New Year's service on 1 January 2011. Twenty-three Copts died and dozens were injured.[11]

These crimes, at the hands of the Muslim majority, are just the beginning. But when a state commits the violence, then government has violated its primary duty.[12] The libertarian political economist Frédéric Bastiat summed up this sentiment in one sentence: "Among the services that we demand of the state, the chief is *security*."[13] And Thomas Jefferson, one of the Founding Fathers of the United States, said, "All, too, will bear in mind this sacred principle: that though the will of the majority is in all cases to prevail, that will to be rightful must be reasonable; that the minority possess their equal rights, which equal law must protect, and to violate would be oppression."

---

[10] See "*Time* Reveals its Shortlist for Person of the Year 2012". This webpage was accessed on 5 January 2013 at <http://newsfeed.time.com/2012/12/18/time-reveals-its-shortlist-for-person-of-the-year-2012/>.

[11] See Reuters, "Egypt church blast death toll rises to 23", 4 January 2011. This article was accessed on 15 November 2012 at <http://www.reuters.com/article/2011/01/04/us-egypt-church-idUSTRE7010M020110104>.

[12] For more information about governments and their roles, see Tadros, RC 2013, *The War of the Words: Oppression, Egypt's Copts, and the State*, Proton Writing Consultants Pty Ltd, Sydney. This book was downloaded on 6 May 2013 from <http://www.amazon.com/The-War-Words-Oppression-ebook/dp/B00CMHMCXC/ref=pd_rhf_gw_p_t_1_PNP6>.

[13] See Bastiat, F 1996, *Economic Sophisms*, Foundation for Economic Education, New York.

Yet the Egyptian State, whose charge is to protect the Christian minority (roughly 10 per cent of Egypt's population) from the Muslim majority, has been wilfully failing to uphold its duty of care.[14] Even more disturbing, the Egyptian State has been actively engaging in its own atrocities against the Christians of Egypt. For instance, on 9 October 2011, at least 26 Copts were murdered and more than 300 were injured in downtown Cairo in what became known as the *Maspero Massacre*—a bloodbath coordinated by the Egyptian State and its armed forces.[15] But this is just one example taken from an ever-lengthening list of offences, which the Egyptian State is continuing to inflict on its minorities.

To counter these evils, Copts all over the world are forming organisations to fight on behalf of their shackled brothers and sisters still living in Egypt. Perhaps Jefferson's saying captures the essence of such movements: "All tyranny needs to gain a foothold is for people of good conscience to remain silent." And, in this spirit, the voice of good conscience has stirred a small yet active group of Sydney-based Copts to create the Australian Coptic Movement Association (ACM).

Although the ACM's members organise different humanitarian activities, they mainly strive to enlighten the public about Egypt's Copts and their struggles. They achieve this using many methods: writing newsletters, coordinating protests, giving public talks, distributing press releases, and lobbying politicians and community leaders.

But, for all their efforts, the ACM lacks one vital public-enlightenment tool—a book chronicling Coptic culture and political events in Egypt.

A book can help to inform and inspire. A book can be sent to a local councillor or a member of parliament. A book can edify a child or an adult or an entire community. A book is education. And according to Nelson Mandela, the man who helped demolish the apartheid in

---

[14] According to the CIA's *World Factbook*, Egypt's population is roughly 83.7 million people (July 2012 estimate). About 90 per cent of the people are Muslim (mostly Sunni); 9 per cent, Coptic Christian; and 1 per cent, other Christian. So, at 10 per cent of the population, Christians form a minority. This information was accessed on 18 November 2012 at <https://www.cia.gov/library/publications/the-world-factbook/geos/eg.html>.

[15] See the United States Commission on International Religious Freedom, "2012 Annual Report". This report was accessed on 18 November 2012 at <http://www.uscirf.gov/reports-and-briefs/annual-report/3706-2012-annual-report.html>.

South Africa, "Education is the most powerful weapon that you can use to change the world."

So the concept for this book was planted. It happened during a lunchtime café meeting, which I participated in with three dedicated and untiring members of the ACM: Peter Tadros, Anthony Hanna, and Sarah Ramsay. The unanimous decision? Through education, we shall free the Copts.

Ideas—alone—do not shape a book, though. It demands hard work. As a consequence, the words coalesced through the toil of many writers and contributors. These generous souls sacrificed their time and energy to raise awareness of how Egypt mistreats its minorities. And these contributors asked for nothing in return. As Jefferson would say, they are people of good conscience who refuse to remain silent and let tyranny gain a foothold.

Each chapter in this book represents a different writer's ideas. Depending on their expertise or knowledge, a few authors have focused on Coptic culture or history, whereas others have concentrated on politics or the push for legal equality in Egypt. Yet, woven together, these various insights and personal pleas have shaped a unique book. It is a compendium of Coptic culture, by Coptic advocates, for Coptic justice.

The Coptic Orthodox Christians are the original people of Egypt. They are the true descendants of the Ancient Egyptians. Once were pharaohs, now the Copts are subjugated in their own homeland—and they have been under siege since the Muslim conquest of Egypt (639–642 AD).

Today, there are even Islamist whispers demanding the destruction of Ancient Egyptian monuments: the Sphinx, the Pyramids, and all pharaonic artefacts.[16] If the extremists can wipe out Egypt's history—its Ancient Egyptian and Coptic history—then perhaps they can obliterate all traces of its original people.

Perhaps. Perhaps not. It all depends on whether people of good conscience remain silent or take a stand against tyranny.

Will Egypt's Coptic Christians continue to suffer in silence? Or shall the world hear their story?

---

[16] See CNN, "Extremist calls for destruction of Egyptian antiquities", 13 November 2012. This article was accessed on 21 November 2012 at <http://edition.cnn.com/2012/11/12/world/wedeman-ancient-monuments/index.html>.

~~~~~~

Ramy Christopher Tadros *is the author of* The War of the Words: Oppression, Egypt's Copts, and the State *and* The Writer's Manifesto: Rules for Writing with Class.

Tadros has researched and written parliamentary documents for various Australian Commonwealth Government departments. He now writes and edits nonfiction for a living, and is the director of Proton Writing Consultants Pty Ltd <http://www.writersmarke.com>, an Australian-based writing, editing, and publishing company.

Tadros also teaches writing and editing courses at Sydney Community College.

Although Tadros likes playing with words and styling suave sentences, he also enjoys politics and economics and is pursuing postgraduate research in political economy. But, come to think of it, politics and economics are still connected with word play.

2. THE COPTS, THE WEST, AND "SYMBOLIC ANNIHILATION"

Peter Day

The Harvard scholar Leila Ahmed recalls in her autobiography, *Border Passage*, the period when a new definition of national identity was imposed on Egyptians by the military dictatorship that arrived in 1952, courtesy of Colonel Gamal Abdel Nasser. Ahmed was at that time a 12-year-old schoolgirl in Cairo, and remembers the constant drumbeat of the government-controlled media: "*Al-qawmiyya al-Arabiyya! Al-Uraba! Nahnu al-Arab!* Arab nationalism! Arabness! We the Arabs!"

Egyptians had never experienced anything like it. "The moment one turned on the radio," Ahmed recalls, "there it was: military songs, and endless, endless speeches in that frenetic, crazed voice of exhortation. In public places, in the street, it filled the air, blaring at one from the grocery, the newsstand, the café, the garage, for it became patriotic to have it on at full volume."

This mass indoctrination in the racial ideology of Arabism was to be of profound significance for Egypt, says Ahmed, because it "unsettled and undercut the old understanding of who we were and silently excluded people who had been included in the old definition of Egyptian." Among these people were the Copts, who, she says,

were Copts precisely because they had refused to convert to the religion of the Arabs and had refused, unlike us Muslims, to intermarry with Arabs. As a result, Copts (members of the ancient Christian church of Egypt) were the only true indigenous inhabitants of Egypt and as such, in our home anyway and in the notion of Egypt with which I grew up, Copts had a very special place in the country.[17]

Nasser's "definition of us" as essentially Arab changed all that. From then on, says Ahmed, there was a feeling in Egypt that Copts were "no longer at the heart" of what it meant to be an Egyptian.

Historical accounts of the pre-Nasser, liberal constitutional era, lasting roughly from the First World War era to the early 1950s, confirm that Professor Ahmed's understanding of the Copts' "special place" during that period is accurate. Egyptians who had won a large measure of independence in their 1919 revolution against British control were justly proud of their new liberal constitution, democratic elections, and free press, as well as their country's steady economic progress and growing middle class. They were also proud of the diversity of the country's religious and ethnic minorities.

That generation identified their emerging, now formally independent modern nation, with the legacy and symbolism of the ancient Egyptian Pharaonic civilisation. *Egyptianism* or *Pharaonism*, as it was sometimes called, affirmed a unique cultural identity, while offering symbols of national unity that were embraced by Muslims and Christians alike.

Pharaonism also had immense cultural appeal, inspiring a flood of novels, plays, musicals, paintings, and sculptures, as well as fashions, furnishings, and architectural styles, and even the themes of the first film offerings from what would grow into a major Egyptian movie industry. The sensational uncovering of the glittering wonders of King Tutankhamen's tomb, which coincided almost to the day with the opening of the first parliament under Egypt's new liberal constitution, just seemed to confirm the inevitability of it all.

Although Pharaonism bestowed a certain prestige on the Copts, as recalled by Leila Ahmed, this was no obstacle to its enthusiastic adoption by the Muslim liberal leaders of the time. But in the 1930s, under the pressure of economic hardship and political extremism, the "golden age" politics of modernisation and tolerance that went under the banner of Pharaonism began to sour—much as liberal democracy began to sour in Europe at the same time and for similar reasons.

---

[17] Ahmed, L 2000, *A Border Passage: from Cairo to America—a woman's journey*, Penguin, p. 244.

It was in the political street gangs of that period that the young Nasser's ambitions began to take shape. The growth of the Muslim Brotherhood, whose political philosophy and organising methods were also heavily influenced by the thriving European totalitarian movements of the time, was accompanied by increasingly shrill demands for the subordination of Egypt to sharia *and* to an international, overarching pan-Islamic rule.

The Brotherhood's founder, Hasan al-Banna, derided Pharaonism as a movement whose aim was "to annihilate the characteristic traits of Islam and Arabism". And he ridiculed the Pharaonist notion of Egypt as a unique territorial nation with a pride-inspiring ancient historical legacy. This, he said, was an "abysmally deep contradiction" with the Islamic ideal of a universal community of Muslims—an *umma* that recognised no borders. Such rhetoric was accompanied from the late 1930s by increasingly violent attacks on Copts, especially in Upper Egypt where they were most concentrated.[18]

But it was only with Nasser's 1952 coup, which the Brotherhood supported at the time, that the old inclusive Pharaonist Egypt was finally swept away. This meant the loss of a constitutional monarchy and an entire liberal order, including a freely elected democratic parliament. Nasser's Minister of Culture sternly instructed Egyptian historians, "The history of modern Egypt begins on 23 July 1952. It has no modern history before then." Histories of the pre-Nasser era soon vanished from bookstores.[19]

Historical research covering the pre-Islamic "Coptic" centuries of Egyptian history suffered a similar fate. Even some radical leftists of Coptic background, who had been Nasser's supporters, complained. For example, Anouar Abdel-Malek (who died in June 2012) noted in his book on the Nasser regime that the school curriculum was "completely ignoring six centuries of Coptic history".[20] Another Coptic leftist intellectual, Ghali Shukri, was "astonished" that in schools,

---

[18] Wood, M 1998, "The Use of the Pharaonic Past in Modern Egyptian Nationalism", *Journal of the American Research Center in Egypt*, vol. 35, pp. 179–196.

[19] Gorman, A 2003, *Historians, state and politics in twentieth century Egypt*, RoutledgeCurzon, London, p. 53.

[20] Abdel-Malek, A 1968, *Egypt, military society*, Random House, p. 261.

literature, and the media "we do not recognize a Coptic Egypt, that is, a Christian Egypt, an Egyptian Egypt."

Shukri said he found it even more astonishing, because "what has survived [from] Coptic Egypt ... are people who live among us like an authentic scarlet thread in the weave of the Egyptian nation". He also said it were "as if the Islamic conquest was the beginning of the history of Egypt, and the non-Muslims are the uninvited guests of this history."[21]

From there, of course, the situation has only deteriorated, especially since the rule of Sadat in the 1970s, when Islamists were enabled to take control of dominant positions in Egypt's educational institutions.

Sadly, the situation does not seem much better in the Middle Eastern studies departments of many Western universities. This is of particular significance, because Western correspondents writing about foreign affairs for the major media are usually graduates of those universities. That is to say, they have been trained in the heartland of political correctness, where it continues to be enforced with ever-greater ferocity. As a consequence, intellectual timidity and careerism reign supreme.

The late Edward Said, whose book *Orientalism* is regarded as the founding text of the post-colonialism that for 30 years has influenced Middle Eastern studies and beyond, once pronounced that any interest in these minorities might be used as a cover for advancing imperialist interests. Fear of such pervasive "hermeneutics of suspicion" explains why the recent history and contemporary situation of the Copts, the largest Christian minority in the Middle East, are largely ignored in the academies. (Paul Rowe, a Canadian academic working in this field, puts it down to fear of "divisiveness".)[22]

This situation has, however, been brewing even longer than the revolution in Middle Eastern studies that followed the appearance of Said's book in 1978. That, it seems, was a revolution waiting to happen. As early as 1972, Maxime Rodinson, a French historian of the Middle East, observed that "the anti-colonial left, whether Christian or not,

---

[21] Gorman, p. 153.

[22] Rowe, PS 2010, "The Middle Eastern Christian as Agent", *International Journal of Middle East Studies,* vol. 42. The Edward Said reference is from Said, *Covering Islam,* as cited in Paul Rowe. Rowe, PS 2001, "Four guys and a fax machine? New Information technology and the internationalization of Religion in Egypt", *Journal of Church and State,* vol. 43(1), pp. 81–92.

often goes so far as to sanctify Islam and the contemporary ideologies of the Muslim world. ... Understanding has given way to apologetics pure and simple." As a life-long Marxist, Rodinson knew well whereof he spoke.[23]

Recent university funding scandals in the United Kingdom and the United States relating to the Libyan Gaddafi regime, such as its "partnering" activities with the London School of Economics, drew renewed attention to the vast sums of money that since the 1970s have poured out of Saudi Arabia and the Gulf to finance chairs in Middle East studies at Western universities or even whole new academic departments, "centres of excellence", and the like. It seems that many academics in the field have simply gone with the flow.

One European practitioner explains what appears at first glance, anyway, to be an entire theory of history writing based on the principle of going along to get along—no doubt with the best will in the world. Writing in the *International Journal of Middle East Studies*, specifically about Christian history in the Middle East, Bernard Heyberger of the *Ecole Pratique des Hautes Etudes* in Paris instructs his international colleagues as follows: "The work of the historian ... is a work of keeping the events at a distance, of rendering them harmless by building a rational discourse around them that offers a vision of the past that will be *acceptable to everyone*" (my emphasis).[24]

Everyone? A survey of the relevant literature suggests that Copts, at least, are seen by many as more or less fair game. Indeed, some future Middle Eastern correspondent now studying at an Ivy League university might at this moment be learning that "Coptic identity" is a mere "construction" emerging from "the colonial era and western fantasies of the Pharaohs".[25] (Those words are copied from a Princeton PhD dissertation, which is respectfully referenced and quoted in academic literature such as the recently published volume *Religious Minorities in the Middle East: Domination, Self-Empowerment, Accommodation*.)[26]

[23] Rodinson, M 1974, *The Legacy of Islam*, Oxford, p. 59.

[24] Heyberger, B 2010, "Eastern Christians, Islam, and the West: A Connected History", roundtable, *International Journal of Middle East Studies*, vol. 42 (3).

[25] Oram, E 2004, "Constructing modern Copts: The production of Coptic Christian identity in contemporary Egypt", dissertation, Princeton University.

[26] Longva, AN & Roald, AS 2012, eds, *Religious Minorities in the Middle East: Domination, Self-Empowerment, Accommodation*, Brill.

In another recent academic article on the Copts, published in a volume titled *Religious Origins of Nations?: The Christian Communities of the Middle East*, Professor Jacques van der Vliet warns readers in the first sentence that the "typical Coptic identity discourse" is "a by-product of the Orientalism so forcefully denounced by Edward Said". By invoking the name of Said in such emphatic fashion, the author is, of course, implying that the reader should be prepared to denounce it, too.[27]

But Said is hardly an appropriate model for considering the situation of the Copts, or any other Middle Eastern Christians, whose existence he scarcely acknowledged, despite having spent most of his childhood and adolescence in Egypt (where he was educated at the elite, British-established Victoria College).

Ibn Warraq, an independent scholar who has written an entire book for the single purpose of eviscerating Said's *Orientalism*, has noticed that in Said's version of the Middle East, "non-Muslims, and even non-Arabs, hardly exist ... [and] are never discussed or acknowledged as Orientals with a history and presence." Said's Middle East is a land where "there are no Copts, no Maronites, no Mandaeans, no Samaritans, no Assyrians, no Greek Orthodox Christians, no Chaldeans, no Berbers, and of course no Jews." It is a place "peopled with Arabs and Muslims on the one hand and 'all the others' on the other hand". But these "others" are never to be considered part of that capitalised "Other" with which we are all now so familiar.[28]

If we were to adopt the terminology of feminist studies, and apply it to the scholarly treatment of the Copts in most Middle Eastern studies departments, the appropriate phrase to use would be "symbolic annihilation". But, of course, feminist terminology raises another issue. For as the Australian feminist author Ida Lichter recently observed in *The Australian* and America's *Huffington Post*, some feminists are choosing to ignore the horrors being perpetrated by Islamist regimes, and are thereby "disregarding the oppression of women and homosexuals". Dr Lichter seems to know how to bell that cat: she says they are doing so "in favour of overarching aims to rid the world of colonialism, neo-colonialism and capitalism".[29]

---

[27] van der Vliet, J 2009, "The Copts: 'Modern Sons of the Pharaohs'?", *Church History & Religious Culture*, vol. 89 (1–3), pp. 279–290.

[28] Warraq, I 2007, *Defending the West: a critique of Edward Said's Orientalism*, Prometheus Books.

This is yet another testament to the truth of some observations on this point by Bassam Tibi, a Muslim scholar of Syrian background. Tibi, who is also a former 1960s radical leftist graduate of Germany's Frankfurt School, recalls the time when "liberal and left-wing humanists who dared to criticize Soviet Communist practices that violated human rights had to run the risk of being accused of 'anti-Communism'." He charges that, in one respect at least, nothing has really changed: "the left engages in a similar terminological policing today in order to censor any free and critical discussion ... about Islamism and its violations of individual human rights."

Despite this, it has been good to see, over the past couple of years, some much improved coverage of the Copts' plight in the main Western media. It is needed now, more than ever. I was in Egypt at the time of the Alexandria church bombing early on New Years Day, 2011, when I reported for *The Spectator* magazine the terrible presentiment of Hani Shukrallah, managing editor of *Al-Ahram*. On that New Years Day, he wrote the following column:

> It is not easy to empty Egypt of its Christians, [because] they've been here for as long as there has been Christianity in the world. ... Yet now, two centuries after the birth of the modern Egyptian nation state ... the previously unheard of seems no longer beyond imagining: a Christian-free Egypt.

The fall of Mubarak shortly after the Alexandria atrocity was, of course, accompanied by an upwelling of renewed hope. But the ominous portents have not receded. Since that time, scores of Copts have been shot, wounded, maimed, or imprisoned. Churches have been torched or torn down. Homes have been burned. Girls have been abducted.

Rather than bring the perpetrators to justice, though, an Egyptian court has now issued death sentences against Copts living abroad, who reportedly had nothing to do with a supposedly offending video, but who have dared to protest against the attacks on their co-religionists in Egypt. These people are citizens of Western democracies, which raises a question: why are their governments so craven that they remain silent on a foreign power's open threats to the lives of their citizens, who have committed no crime?

---

[29] Lichter, I 2012 "Feminists betray Islamic women", *Huffington Post*, 24 October.

Nearly half of Egypt's population voted against the Islamist candidate Mohamed Morsi in the 2012 presidential election. Since the day on which President Morsi claimed the rights of a dictator, it is certain many more have turned against him. The anti-Islamists now risking their lives on Egyptian streets are standing up for all the people. But Morsi's chief international sponsor, the US Government, is nonetheless supplying his regime with 16 F-16 fighter jets, 200 tanks, and 140,000 canisters of tear gas. Perhaps this is just another example of the United States "leading from behind". In any case, it is now clearly up to the rest of the civilised world to support those whose only crime is to object to living under an Islamist dictatorship.

Hani Shukrallah's warning continues to echo ominously.

~~~~~~

Peter Day, a former Washington correspondent for The Australian *newspaper, has travelled extensively in Egypt over many years. He has written for* The Spectator *and* Quadrant *on the Mubarak Regime and its aftermath, and is now writing a book on Egypt, the West, and the "Arab Spring".*

3. EGYPT AND THE COPTS

Lord David Alton

For two millennia, Christians have been woven into the fabric of the Middle East. Yet, as Pope Benedict XVI has warned, "Churches in the Middle East are threatened in their very existence."

The ancient churches of the region, of which the Coptic Church is the largest, have contributed enormously to the rich story of Christianity. But we who are privileged to live in free societies that enjoy religious freedom and freedom of speech seem ignorant of and indifferent to the fate of Christians living in the lands of Christianity's birth.

From the religion's humble origins in a Bethlehem stable to the stunning wonders of Byzantium, and from the beautiful liturgies of the Chaldeans, Marionites, Syrianis, Copts, and other ancient Christian traditions to the evangelism of contemporary converts who risk their lives by committing the crime of apostasy, the story of the Middle East's Christians is one of persecution and suffering—of which we are too frequently ignorant or silent.

Between 2011 and 2012, however, the crisis facing the ancient churches has deepened.

Palestinian Christians now constitute just 0.5 per cent of the population; in Lebanon, they have declined from 75 per cent to 32 per cent. They have faced asphyxiation in Iraq, persecution in Saudi Arabia, execution in Iran, and share in the terrors of Syria. In the 1987 census, there were 1.4 million Christians living in Iraq; today, there may be fewer than 150,000. This exodus has been of biblical proportions. As one Christian source in Iraq comments, "The attacks on Christians continue, and the world remains totally silent. It's as if we have been swallowed up by the night."

The region's biggest Christian population is in Egypt—and they joined with Muslim neighbours in the heady pro-democracy demonstrations in Tahrir Square. But the Christians had barely taken their banners home before Salafi groups began to foment sectarian violence against the Copts. The Egyptian Muslim novelist Alaa Al-Aswany put it well when he said, "We can expect Islamists to use the democratic system merely as a ladder to power, which they will climb up and then kick away so that no one else can use it."

More than 100,000 Coptic Christians left Egypt over a nine-month period last year, and they were coerced into that, according to the director of the European Union of Human Rights Organisations, "by threats and intimidation of hard-line Salafists, and by the lack of protection they are getting from the Egyptian regime".

Syria's bishop of Aleppo, Bishop Audo, flags up the significance of a Middle East without Christians and is firm in his conviction that Arab Christians provide a vital contribution for the whole Middle East region:

> If the presence of Christians continues to decline, the impact will be felt far and wide. It will not just be a loss to the Christians, but it will be a loss to the Muslims. The Muslims need the presence of Christians as a safeguard to ensure their true identity is maintained. Christians are like them in so many ways, and at the same time are yet different. Hence, the Christians are well placed to help Muslims keep their bearings as a faith community centred on belief in one God and tolerance for others.

This urgent need for tolerance is underlined by what occurred in Alexandria, Egypt, at the beginning of 2011. Christian worshippers had been attending the Midnight Mass at the Coptic Church of the Two Saints in Alexandria, when radical Islamists left a trail of destruction, death, and injury.

I was particularly struck by something which Amira Nowaira, a Muslim, wrote about the carnage. Describing the changing nature of Egyptian society, she recounted two stories that sum up the alternative paths that Egypt can take: one is built on cultivating a civilised respect

17

and tolerance of difference, whereas the other rests on violence, uncivilised intolerance, and hatred of difference. One is about unfulfilled hope; the other, about loss.

Nowaira's first story concerned a young Coptic woman called Mariam "Mariouma" Fekry, who on the last day of 2010 entered the following note on Facebook:

[The year] 2010 is over. ... This year has the best memories of my life. ... Really enjoyed living this year. ... I hope 2011 is much better. ... I have so many wishes in 2011. ... Hope they come true. ... Please God stay beside me and help make it all [come] true.

Just hours after writing her message, Mariam was among those killed in Alexandria—along with her mother, her aunt, and her younger sister, Martina.

Nowaira's second story concerned herself. She described how

As a child growing up in a traditional Muslim family in the 60s, I remember quite clearly after suffering a bout of illness that conventional medicine seemed unable to cure, my mother took me to an Orthodox church in the popular district of Moharrem Bek to light a candle in honour of the Virgin Mary. As we stood together in the beautifully decorated and darkly lit church, my mother, an ordinary, middle-class woman, whispered some heartfelt prayers. She didn't feel that she was on alien territory, or that she was in any way betraying her faith in appealing to the Christian God to heal her daughter. This simple and spontaneous act of reverence seems sadly unthinkable in today's Egypt.

The violence that robbed Mariam, her sister, her mother, and her aunt of their lives—and the subsequent violence at Maspero—and the loss of the innocent coexistence described by Nowaira are all part of the festering story that characterises Egypt today.

The failure of the international community to champion the Copts and other ancient churches clearly has implications for girls like Mariam—but it also has implications for the region and for us.

Speaking about the silence of so many in the face of Hitler's depredations, the Protestant theologian Dietrich Bonhoeffer, who was executed by the Nazis, said, "We have been the silent witnesses of evil deeds." In our generation we, too, have been silent witnesses as the Middle East's Christians have faced significantly intensified persecution and violence.

Although the Copts have suffered a wide range of persecution and discrimination for centuries, for much of the time many Muslims and Christians were able to coexist peacefully. What has changed, today, is that with the arrival of radical Islamic ideas, and calls for an exclusively Islamic state, Christian groups are confronted with higher risks and face constant persecution, despite constitutional protections.

Even before the protests in Tahrir Square and the turbulence that accompanied Mubarak's fall, the attacks had increased in frequency and severity, while the attackers have enjoyed immunity from prosecution. The current campaign of persecution and violation of the human rights of Egypt's Copts have included extortion, bigotry, discrimination, the confiscation of property, the siege of some towns, the imposition of unjust laws, the murdering of civilians in their churches and in broad daylight, and even the bombing and torching of churches—all accompanied by the curse of impunity.

And who can forget what happened on 9 October 2011? On this day, moderate Muslims joined with their Coptic neighbours and marched through Cairo's Maspero area to protest the burning of a Coptic church; however, during the march, radicals wielding sticks and swords attacked the unarmed protestors. And the Egyptian security forces—after they rammed armed vehicles into the Coptic crowd and fired live ammunition at them—soon prohibited media coverage and tried to remove the evidence. At least 26 people were killed in the massacre, and more than 300 were injured. Maspero was Egypt's worst sectarian violence in 60 years.

It is 20 years since I wrote a report for the Jubilee Campaign on the plight of the Copts. It was based on firsthand accounts and evidence, which was collected during a visit to Egypt. I quoted Pope Shenouda III of Alexandria, who reminded the world that the ancient Coptic community is not made up of foreigners in a strange land: "Egypt is not a country we live in but a country that lives within us."

Back in 1992 I wrote that

Insecurity and fear remain the most crucial and pressing concerns. The same ugly phenomenon of ethnic cleansing that happened in Bosnia—the destruction of the culture and civilisation of minorities and their vilification—is to be found in the villages of Upper Egypt. Christian women have been raped; men and their families have been induced or pressurised in their thousands to convert to Islam. Local police officers have either ignored the attacks or have collaborated.

The US Department of State referred to this continuing pattern of persecution in its *2010 Report on International Religious Freedom*: "The status of respect for religious freedom by the government remained poor, unchanged from the previous year."

Nothing much has changed in the underlying situation. Yet the gaping wounds are now more openly on display. On satellite channels, for instance, fanatical preachers have been allowed to incite hatred and target non-Muslims. And it is a cruel irony that a Government, which prosecutes journalists and writers who criticise Government policies, does nothing to prosecute those who are responsible for stirring hatred and making unfounded and dangerously inflammatory statements— including suggestions that Copts have been amassing weapons and creating a secret army. Such comments are obviously designed to incite further hatred and bitterness.

Coptic women have also been targeted. Over the years, hundreds of young Christian girls have been abducted from their families and raped. They are then forced to convert to Islam and marry Muslim men. And the State has done little to support Coptic parents seeking the return of their abducted daughters. It is hard to believe this is happening in twenty-first-century Egypt, a country that takes pride in being a member of the United Nations Human Rights Council.

The radicalisation of Egyptian society, says Nowaira, "is now visually present on our streets and in our public spaces, not only in women's attire but also in the large number of men wearing their beards long in an ostentatious display of their religious creed."

The Arab Spring must be viewed against this backdrop of radicalisation and long-term victimisation of Egypt's Copts. Egypt has tried to silence those tolerant members of its Muslim community who speak out against the mistreatment and unjust policies—even going so far as to imprison its own citizens when they have attempted to defend the rights of Christian groups.

Those moderate Muslims—like Amira Nowaira—understand that if a country were to treat its minorities well, then through these actions that country would mould a decent society for the majority. Those moderate Muslims know that if a country were to disrespect the human rights of minorities, then the human rights of the majority would also be ignored. And those moderate Muslims understand that if a country were to elevate religious freedom, then that country would increase its charitable works and enhance the common good for all society.

The 2011 Alexandria bombing is a warning for President Mohamed Morsi—and the West.

Will Egypt become a nation for all its citizens—or just for some? Will it be a nation that focuses on a person's religious or political beliefs—or on a citizen's willingness and ability to contribute? Will it be a nation where all men and women are treated equally and justly before the law? Will it be a society that promotes an authentic citizenship for all its citizens rather than one based on religious and political apartheid and discrimination of second-class *dhimmis?* Will Egypt protect the rights of its religious minorities against those who incite violence or preach hatred against them?

On the answers to those questions turns the fate of the Copts—and the right of Egypt to count itself among the civilised nations of the world.

~~~~~~

Professor Lord David Alton *is the honorary president of UK Copts and the co-founder of the Jubilee Campaign. He served in the British House of Commons for 18 years, and has been an independent member of the House of Lords since 1997. For more information about his work, please visit <http://www.davidalton.net>.*

4. RELIGIOUS FREEDOM IN EGYPT: RECOMMENDATIONS FOR U.S. POLICY

Dr Katrina Lantos Swett[30]

I want to thank Mr Adel Guindy and Coptic Solidarity for giving me the opportunity to speak briefly this afternoon about the status of religious freedom in Egypt and the recommendations our Commission is offering to address this serious situation.

Since its inception nearly 15 years ago, the United States Commission on International Religious Freedom (USCIRF) has been deeply engaged on Egypt, and for good reason: for our entire existence, and indeed, prior to our creation, religious freedom conditions, including those of Egypt's Coptic population, have been extremely concerning.

From the evidence we have seen, the biggest problem faced by the Copts continues to be one of impunity. Simply stated, for decades, Egypt's government has fostered a climate conducive to acts of violence against Copts and members of other minority communities. It has done so in at least two ways.

First, Cairo's long history of restrictive laws and policies—from blasphemy codes to an Emergency Law to across-the-board discrimination—has drawn unwelcome attention to religious minorities, further marginalising them and leading to violent words and

---

[30] These remarks were presented by USCIRF Chair Dr Katrina Lantos Swett at the Coptic Solidarity Third Annual Conference on 28 June 2012.

deeds launched by intolerant individuals as well as by radical religious groups.

Second, the Government's continued failure to protect innocent people from these attacks and to convict those responsible has served to encourage further assaults. For years, President Mubarak's government tolerated widespread discrimination against religious minorities and disfavoured religious groups—from dissident Sunni and Shia Muslims to Baha'is, as well as Copts and other Christians—while allowing state-controlled media and state-funded mosques to deliver incendiary messages against them. After Mubarak's departure, however, a breakdown in security and a rise in sectarian violence made 2011 one of the worst years for Copts and other minorities. Last year alone, violent sectarian attacks killed approximately a hundred people, surpassing the death toll of the previous 10 years combined. As during the Mubarak regime, Copts were the primary target, and most of the perpetrators still have not been brought to justice.

This is intolerable.

In October 2011, Egypt's State media falsely accused Copts of attacking the military when Muslim and Christian protestors marched toward the State television station. Following the State media's call for civilians to counter this imaginary threat, on 9 October, in downtown Cairo, armed men attacked peaceful demonstrators, killing at least 26 of them—most of whom were Copts—while injuring over 300 more. Responding to the violence, Egypt's military used live ammunition and also deployed armoured vehicles that deliberately crushed and killed at least 12 protestors.

This is not to say there has been no progress since the end of the Mubarak regime. To be sure, we have seen some hopeful developments. In 2011, the Al-Azhar University in Cairo published statements expressing support for freedom of religion or belief. In May of the same year, the Government began to reopen more than 50 churches that had been closed, in some cases, for years; then, in July, the Supreme Administrative Court ruled that reconverts to Christianity could obtain new national identity documents indicating their Christianity but not their former Muslim faith. And, following the October violence, the transitional Government took steps to reduce discrimination in Egypt's Penal Code.

Yet despite this progress, the bottom line is this: Copts need to be protected, Copts are not being protected, and Copts must be protected—along with every other member of Egyptian society—from attacks on their right to order their lives and practise their beliefs in dignity and peace. So long as Copts and other religious minorities are not being sufficiently protected, USCIRF will continue to spotlight the problem and recommend that the US Government take strong action in support of religious freedom.

Our recommendations to the US Government are as follows:

First, the United States should press Egypt to improve religious freedom conditions by repealing discriminatory decrees against religious minorities, removing religion from official identity documents, abolishing the blasphemy codes, and passing a unified law for the construction and repair of places of worship.

Second, the United States should urge Egypt's Government to prosecute government-funded clerics, government officials, or any other individuals who incite violence, while disciplining or dismissing government-funded clerics who preach intolerance and hatred.

Third, the United States should increase pressure on Egypt to bring to justice those who have committed violence against fellow Egyptians on account of their religion.

Fourth, Washington should press Cairo to include robust protections for religious freedom in a new constitution.

Fifth, the US Congress should require the Departments of State and Defense to report every 90 days on the Egyptian Government's progress pertaining to religious freedom and related rights.

Sixth, until genuine progress occurs, USCIRF renews its call for the United States to designate Egypt a "country of particular concern" as one of the world's most serious religious-freedom abusers.

And, finally, if Egypt demonstrates a commitment to progress on freedom of religion and related rights, the United States should ensure that a portion of its military aid to Egypt be used to help Egypt's police implement a plan to enhance protection for religious minorities and their places of worship.

Today, as Egypt confronts the rigours of democratic transition, will it uphold the rights of Copts and other religious minorities?

The world is watching—and USCIRF is watching, too.

~~~~~~

Dr Katrina Lantos Swett is the chair of the United States Commission on International Religious Freedom (USCIRF), an independent, bipartisan US

Federal Government body dedicated to defending the universal right to freedom of religion or belief abroad. She also serves as the president and chief executive officer of the Lantos Foundation for Human Rights and Justice, which she established in 2008 to carry on the legacy of her father, the late Congressman Tom Lantos, and to support human rights and honour its advocates throughout the world.

Swett is a graduate of Yale University. She earned her JD degree at the University of California, Hastings College of Law, and also holds a PhD in History from the University of Southern Denmark.

5. A LETTER TO THE COPTIC PEOPLE

The Hon. Philip Ruddock

The Coptic community in Australia is a significant, vocal and active community, who have made their home in Australia. Although they are committed Australians, they still remain closely linked to their homeland. Over the years, their contributions to our country have been significant, yet today many are concerned about friends and families back home in Egypt. During this time of change and challenge in Egypt, it is worth taking a moment to look at the history of the Copts and their relationship with Australia into the future.

The Copts are the largest Christian denomination in the Arab world, and trace their heritage back to the earliest days of Christendom when St Mark introduced Egyptians to Christ. Subsequent and rapid growth throughout Egypt saw Christianity at one point forming a majority of Egypt's population. From this high point, however, the rapid and continuous growth of Islam gradually displaced the Copts as the majority.

After the 1952 coup d'état in Egypt, the Copts found themselves increasingly marginalised by what appeared to be semi-official government direction. Certainly, the government exploited community fears and concerns to focus upon the Copts as an "other" within Egyptian society. That marginalisation manifested itself, most commonly, as arson, mob attacks, difficulty in gaining employment, and petty harassment and discrimination. Local disputes between neighbours took on a religious edge over everyday events, like a relationship between a Coptic man and a Muslim woman. Muslims and Christians living in close proximity saw a religious element intensify normal neighbourhood disputes, with some in the government only too keen to exploit religious division.

Events often escalated, flaring up into violence, at the cost of lives. We saw this in the el-Kosheh attacks in 2000 and 2001, which saw 20 Christians killed following a dispute between a Muslim and a Christian. More recently, there was the January 2011 car bombing outside the Two Saints Church in Alexandria, where a bomb was timed to detonate just as congregants were leaving the church. The explosion killed 23 Copts and injured more than 97. And in the turmoil surrounding the fall of the Mubarak regime, violent clashes saw 24 killed and many injured, with divisions between the Muslim and Christian communities exploited. Sadly, violence is becoming an all-too-common part of daily life for the Copts.

Not only have the changes in Egypt's political system caused difficulties, the passing of Pope Shenouda III of Alexandria, the much-loved leader of the Church, has also heightened the uncertainty of the times. For more than 40 years, Pope Shenouda III provided leadership for the community, operating in a fraught political environment to try to protect the Coptic community and its interests. I had the privilege of meeting him in Australia on a number of occasions, and I know well that he was a steadying influence and an effective leader of the church. With his incomparable leadership and experience, he provided a stabilising hand and wise counsel to the Coptic community, in Egypt and abroad. Many in Australia keenly felt his loss, which came at a crucial time. Leadership in a comparatively small church, struggling constantly to maintain cohesion in the face of minority status, is always a challenge—and it was one well understood by Pope Shenouda III.

Pope Tawadros II, the successor of Pope Shenouda III, will face many challenges. Pope Tawadros II will need to find, and maintain, a place for the Coptic community in the new Egypt. With the Copts accounting for 10 per cent of the Egyptian population, this will be a difficult task. The growing strength of the Muslim Brotherhood and other Islamist groups in Egypt will place further pressure on the Copts, as will the new constitution, which discriminates against many minorities.

Providing spiritual and theological leadership, guidance and education, for the Coptic community during these difficult times will be key to Pope Tawadros' ongoing success. He will act as a leader for a people that, in all likelihood, will continue to face persecution and violence for some time yet. He will also have to watch as many of his people leave Egypt, seeking new homes overseas. And many of those will be some of the youngest and most-promising members of the community—the future leaders of the Church and the Coptic community in Egypt. Like many observers, I do not wish to see a situation in which the Coptic Church cannot continue to reside in its ancestral homelands. We, the international community, must continue to work to advance this matter.

During my many years in public life, I have developed close relationships with the clergy and the community of the Coptic Church. I have spent time with Bishop Suriel, Bishop Daniel, and the Very Reverend Father Tadros El-Bakhoumi, and heard their concerns for the Church in Egypt. In my own electorate in Berowra, I have a small Coptic church, St Mary and St Sidhom Bishay, in Galston. For a relatively small expatriate community in Australia, the Copts have proved remarkably cohesive. They are effective in advancing their interests and quick to adapt to their new lives and opportunities.

From an Australian perspective, as Minister for Immigration, I worked to assist, where possible, the resettlement of Copts fleeing oppression, and it has been gratifying to see so many have made Australia their home.

However, it is equally important that we speak out about those Copts remaining in Egypt. Although we need to help secure their safety in the first instance, we must also strive to uphold their freedom to worship and live as they choose in their homelands. Copts should be as free to practise their faith in Egypt as Muslims are free to do so here in Australia.

The expatriate Coptic community is an important part of that struggle for equality, and will continue to raise awareness and embrace activism on behalf of their friends and relatives in Egypt.

I wish Pope Tawadros II the best of luck in his new role, and my thoughts are with the Copts of Egypt as they navigate these precarious times. They should know they have no greater friend than Australia, and the thoughts of the entire Coptic community in Australia is with them daily.

~~~~~~

The Honourable Philip Ruddock, MP, is the Federal Member of Parliament for the division of Berowra, in North Western Sydney. He is currently the Shadow Cabinet Secretary, and has previously served as the Attorney-General and as the Minister for Immigration and Multiculturalism.

6. Ongoing Coptic struggle in Egypt

The Hon. Jim Karygiannis

The history of the Coptic Orthodox Church in Egypt dates back to Ancient Egypt. The Church has made significant contributions to Christendom.

Yet, throughout the ages, the Coptic Church in Egypt has endured persecution.

In recent years, the persecution of Copts in Egypt has become more blatant and, unfortunately, it has become part of the volatile and ever-changing political and social landscape in Egypt. These incidents have shocked not only the worldwide Coptic community, but much of the international community, and have been condemned at the highest levels.

What happens to members of the Coptic Orthodox Christian community in Egypt has an impact on the community in Canada.

As the Member of Parliament who represents the most ethnically diverse federal riding in Canada, I have worked with the Canadian Coptic community for more than two decades. About a decade ago, they came to me to express their concerns about the plight of their brethren in Egypt. I have voiced their concerns to the Government of Canada and urged the Government to press Egyptian authorities to protect the rights of Coptic Orthodox Christians in Egypt. I have also travelled to Egypt on several occasions and seen the hardships suffered by the Coptic Community there.

In 2008, at the request of the Canadian Coptic Association, I led a Liberal Parliamentary delegation to Egypt to look into reports of religious persecution and human rights violations suffered by members of the Coptic community. My colleagues and I met with human rights advocates and academics, who gave us an overview of the geopolitical and economic situation in Egypt at the time and insight into its effect on Coptic Christians. We were also told that there was no differentiation between citizens of Egypt on the part of authorities. However, members of the community described, in some detail, incidents of forced conversions of faith from Christianity to Islam, kidnappings of girls and young women, the destruction of church property, and the feeling that they were being treated differently because of their faith.

Article 40 of the Constitution of the Arab Republic of Egypt, which was suspended following the overthrow of President Hosni Mubarak in February 2011, stated that,

All citizens are equal before the law. They have equal public rights and duties without discrimination between them due to race, ethnic origin, language, religion or creed.

Article 46 of the Constitution stated that,

The State shall guarantee the freedom of belief and the freedom of practicing religious rights.

Canadian Liberal Parliamentarians believed, and continue to believe, that the Government of Canada, as a member of the international community, has an ethical and moral responsibility to assist those whose freedoms are infringed upon.

At the conclusion of this fact-finding trip, the delegation wrote a report that contained the following recommendations:

1. The Canadian Government can assist by:
    —developing programs in Egypt that will promote dialogue and increase tolerance among citizens
    —establishing programs that will increase youth employability after graduation from university
    —ensuring that laws are upheld and that the judicial system is properly sustained.

2. The Canadian Embassy is to hold a dialogue of Interfaith Harmony with a local Egyptian non-governmental organisation (NGO) or educational institution, as well as to provide ongoing assistance to this dialogue.

During this decade, the world has witnessed an escalation in sectarian violence in Egypt. There have been bloody clashes between members of the Coptic and Muslim communities and Egyptian authorities; Coptic churches have been bombed or set on fire; homes and businesses, belonging to Copts, have been destroyed; hundreds of people have been injured or killed, even in peaceful protest; and Coptic Christian mourners have been attacked.

I have issued public statements about these incidents, in which I have conveyed that my thoughts and prayers are with the injured; condemned the barbaric acts of violence; urged the Egyptian authorities to bring the perpetrator or perpetrators to justice; and stressed that the administration of justice not only be fair, but also be seen to be fair.

The attacks on religious minorities in Egypt must stop. The right to practise one's religion in peace is a basic human right. The Egyptian Government must protect all citizens, regardless of religious faith.

Sadly, these unconscionable and reprehensible acts of violence continue.

The Coptic community in Canada watches these and other developments in Egypt with great interest and concern. They want to ensure that Egyptian Christians have equal rights with their fellow Muslim Egyptian citizens with respect to the freedom to practise their faith peacefully.

On several occasions, I have met with members of the Coptic Orthodox Church in Canada, both priests and laity, who have condemned the attacks on innocent Christians. We have also attended memorial services to pray for the souls of those who were killed in violence, pray for the speedy recovery of those injured, and pray for a peaceful and lasting end to the sectarian strife in Egypt.

The religious violence that erupted on 1 January 2011, when al-Qidiseen Coptic Church in Alexandria, Egypt, was bombed and 23 Copts died with more than 100 injured, had serious repercussions for the Coptic Orthodox Christian community around the world. The joy synonymous with the celebration of the Orthodox Christmas on 6 January 2011 was replaced with uneasiness and fear.

Prior to Christmas, Canadian Coptic priests told me of their fear of threats against the Canadian Coptic community, as a list of Canadian Coptic Orthodox Churches and their addresses had been posted on a website affiliated with al-Qaeda. The website also had information on making bombs.

Copts across Canada were anxious about the safety of their community. They demanded the Canadian Government and law enforcement provide security for their churches, so Christmas services could be held in safety. I contacted the Canadian Public Safety Minister and police forces across Canada and conveyed to them the concerns expressed by the clerics. To some extent, security protection was provided.

All Canadians must be able to worship freely and securely.

In June 2012, members of the Canadian Coptic community and I participated in the Third Annual Coptic Solidarity Union Conference in Washington, DC, the United States. This international forum focused on the plight of Egypt's Copts and took place just before Egyptian President Mohamed Morsi assumed office.

In my remarks, I stated that,

> Canada and the rest of the international community are closely watching the President-elect's actions, in these first days of a new government, with great interest. Egypt is embarking on a path toward democracy, and it is important that freedom, freedom of the press, human rights and the protection of the rights of women and religious minorities, including the Coptic community, are protected under the Egyptian Constitution.

The international community, including concerned Canadians of all faiths and walks of life, have condemned the film *Innocence of Muslims* which maligns the Islamic faith.

In my view, the film is hate speech. Denouncing the religious practices of others is wrong and should not be supported anywhere in the world. Freedom of speech is a tenet of democracy; however, it must never be used to incite hatred. The right to worship and observe the tenets of one's faith is a basic right.

In the aftermath of the film's release, the Egyptian Government placed the names of seven Coptic Christians, including two Canadian Coptic Orthodox Christians, on a list for being involved in the production, promotion, and distribution of *Innocence of Muslims*. Jacques Attalla and my constituent, Nader Fawzy, continue to refute these allegations and maintain they have no association whatsoever with the film. They believe they have been targeted, because they are members of the Coptic Orthodox faith and have spoken out against the persecution of Coptic Christians in Egypt.

Both men have sought the protection of local law enforcement. And, since the list was released, I have repeatedly urged the Canadian Government to contact the Egyptian Government about this matter.

On 28 November 2012, the Canadians and the other Egyptian Coptic Christians were convicted and sentenced to death, in absentia, in Cairo. Mr Fawzy is terrified of being kidnapped and spirited to Egypt.

In late 2012, Egyptian President Mohamed Morsi gave himself new absolute powers—changing the Constitution by decree and placing his office above the courts, including the Constitutional Court.

The President's actions precipitated the resignation of Samir Morcos, Presidential Advisor for the Democratic Transition and State Modernization of Egypt. Morcos, who was one of three Coptic Christians on the President's 17-person advisory team, termed the declaration "undemocratic and a leap backwards".

This centralisation of power has alarmed many observers, including the Christian community in Egypt. Canadian Copts organised protest rallies in major centres in Canada, in solidarity with their brethren.

The President had promised a constitution that would be written by the people and represent all the people.

Yet delegates to the Constituent Assembly, representing democratic parties and the Coptic Orthodox and Catholic Churches, ended their participation in writing a new constitution. They boycotted the 16-hour marathon session when more than 230 articles of the draft Constitution were passed, because they believed the Constituent Assembly was failing to represent the Egyptian society in a balanced way.

President Morsi, in a meeting with Pope Tawadros II of Alexandria, told the head of the Coptic Orthodox Church that he was "responsible for safeguarding the rights of all Egyptians without distinction". His Minister of Parliamentary and Legal Affairs assured the Pope that the Coptic Church would remain "part of the homeland and identity of Egypt" regardless of whether its representatives participated in the drafting of the country's new constitution.

As in the previous Egyptian Constitution, the draft Constitution enshrines the principles of sharia.

Article 2 of the draft Constitution states that,

Islam is the religion of the State and Arabic its official language. Principles of Islamic Sharia are the principle source of legislation.

However, Article 43 of the draft Constitution states that,

Freedom of belief is an inviolable right. The State shall guarantee the freedom to practice religious rites and to establish places of worship for the divine religions, as regulated by law.

Freedom of religious practice is limited to the monotheistic religions—Judaism, Christianity, and Islam—which espouse the doctrine that there is only one divine being.

Reaction has been swift and predictable. The international community has voiced concern over the protection of the rights of minorities and women under a new Constitution, and fears exist that Morsi is pushing Egypt into more division and confrontation. There have also been protests and violent confrontations in Egypt between those who support the President and those who oppose these measures.

The international community is closely watching developments in Egypt. There is tremendous concern that what is happening in Egypt, with respect to the Constitution, could marginalise religious minorities and restrict the rights of women and other sectors of the population.

As a concerned Parliamentarian and the Chairman of the Canadian Coptic Parliamentary Friendship Association, I hope and pray that all Egyptians, regardless of faith or political affiliation, can, someday, ease the turmoil that is rocking their country and work together to build a lasting democracy.

As Egypt continues to find its way on the path to democracy, it is important that freedom of the press, human rights, and the protection of the rights of women and religious minorities, including the Coptic community, are preserved under the Egyptian Constitution.

Democracy is messy, and there will, from time to time, be roadblocks and detours that will have to be negotiated.

Through it all, the triumphs and the tribulations, I think it is important to keep in mind the following motto: RACE stands for Respecting our neighbours, Accepting our differences, Celebrating our rich diversity, and Embracing our heritage. We are all part of the human race.

~~~~~~

The Honourable Jim Karygiannis *is a Liberal Member of Parliament for Scarborough-Agincourt in Canada and Liberal Critic for Multiculturalism.*

Karygiannis represents the most ethnically diverse federal riding in Canada. He is an effective voice for the people he serves, and takes their concerns on many issues—including immigration, taxation, justice, and Canada's global responsibilities—to Caucus and the House of Commons for debate.

Karygiannis is also the Chairman of the Canadian Coptic Parliamentary Friendship Association.

7. THE MARTYR COPTIC ORTHODOX CHURCH OF ST MARK

The Rev. the Hon. Fred Nile

The martyr Coptic Orthodox Church of Saint Mark has made one of the most important contributions to the history of the Christian Church from the first century, in spite of continuous periods of persecution right up to the twenty-first century in the nation of Egypt.

The faithful, peaceful, gentle Coptic Christians have been persecuted by the most ruthless forces over the centuries, commencing with the Roman Empire and then the Islamic Ottoman Empire, which treated Coptic Christians as second-class citizens.

Now, in this century, the Coptic Christians are being persecuted by a reinvigorated militant Islamic force led by the fanatical Muslim Brotherhood. Coptic Christians and priests are being murdered, and their churches are being burnt and destroyed. For Coptic Christians, the anticipated *Arab Spring* in the Middle East has turned into the *Arab Winter*, with political power in the hands of Islamic, fundamentalist Muslims.

Pope Shenouda III of Alexandria

I have a powerful memory of my visit to Egypt when I was a guest of the Coptic Church. I had previously visited Egypt in 1966 when I led a delegation to Ireland.

I was humbled to be invited to the Coptic Church in Cairo to attend the weekly Bible study led by Pope Shenouda III, who had me sit on the platform with him. I still remember the Jesus-like exposition of the Gospel, especially the teaching of Jesus Christ where he taught "love your enemies".

The Coptic Christians have practised these teachings for more than 20 centuries and have received bloody persecution in return.

Coptic monasteries

A bishop of the Coptic Church arranged for me to inspect a number of Coptic monasteries located in the desert areas.

I noticed that, because of persecution in the early centuries, the Coptic monks had to build their monasteries in the style of a fort with strong walls to protect them from barbarian attacks. As there were no moats, they had to build strong walls with a bridge that could be raised to the final protected tower in the centre of the monastery.

I was also impressed by the devotion of the monks in their loving care of the relics of previous saints.

Drug rehabilitation programme

When I visited their rehabilitation centre, I was impressed with the Coptic Church's rehabilitation programmes for drug addicts, where they used faith, hard work, and loving care to cure these drug addicts.

Australian experience

I thank God for the warm fellowship I have enjoyed with the Coptic bishops, priests, congregations, and various parishes.

My first contact with the Coptic Church in Sydney occurred when I was invited to one of the earliest Coptic Churches at Sydenham, near Mascot Airport, because they supported my strong Christian witness for Christian values, marriage, and the family.

I was very impressed with the Coptic Liturgy, which was very new to me, and I was surprised when the priest invited me to speak to the congregation. What a privilege—perhaps also because my surname is *Nile?*

Over the years I have been warmly invited to Coptic parishes in Sydney and asked to address the congregations of Bexley, Arncliffe, and Rhodes, among others.

These personal invitations meant a great deal to me, especially when I developed a warm friendship with the first Coptic Bishop in Sydney—Bishop Daniel, who was originally from Sudan. He warmly welcomed me and urged the congregations to support my mission in the NSW Parliament. He was even brave enough to recommend that they should vote for me! I was sorry when he returned to Egypt for a period, but I am pleased that he is once again the Coptic Bishop of Sydney.

I have developed a close friendship with another Coptic bishop, Bishop Daniel of the Pope Shenouda Monastery at Putty, New South Wales. And I was pleased to be a VIP guest at the installation of Bishop Daniel at the monastery.

I have also enjoyed the privilege of being invited to speak at Coptic colleges, which have an impressive education programme for the hundreds of Coptic students.

Orthodox orthodoxy

As an "orthodox" Christian who believes in the biblical teaching, the Apostles' Creed, and the fundamental doctrines of the Christian faith, I have greatly valued and appreciated the biblical orthodoxy of the Coptic Orthodox Church.

They believe in the essentials of the Christian faith, such as the Virgin Birth, the miracles of Jesus Christ, and the Passion of Jesus Christ when He died on the Cross of Calvary and shed His Blood to wash away our sins so that we could be as white as snow "according to the foreknowledge of God the Father, in sanctification of the Spirit, for obedience and sprinkling of the blood of Jesus Christ" (1 Peter 1b). The Copts also believe in His perfect sinless life, His bodily physical resurrection, and His coming again in power and might.

Such orthodox teaching has been vital, when a few other non-orthodox churches have adopted modernism, which rejects and modifies these historic doctrines.

Practical assistance

I have been pleased to assist Coptic parishes to secure property in Sydney suburbs, which is difficult because there is no empty land.

I found a way of approaching the Government and releasing NSW Department of Education school land (which was no longer required by the Department) to provide land for a Coptic church. I was pleased to see the door opening for the Coptic cathedral at Bexley and the parish church at Rhodes.

Coptic church growth

As a result of the growth of the Coptic Church in Australia, there are now two Australian dioceses: one based in Sydney, where there are more than 70,000 Copts, and the other in Melbourne, where there are many thousands of Copts.

May the Lord continue to bless the Coptic Church in Australia, which has come as a reinforcement in the spiritual battle to preserve our Australian Christian heritage and character.

We continue to pray for our oppressed Coptic brothers, sisters, and clergy in Egypt and other lands, where they suffer bloody persecution.

~~~~~~

The Reverend the Honourable Fred Nile, MLC, is the Parliamentary Leader of the Christian Democratic Party and the Member and Assistant President of the Legislative Council, New South Wales State Parliament, Sydney, Australia. He is a long-time advocate of Coptic rights and has passed many motions in Parliament over the past 30 years concerning the Copts.

8. COPTIC STRUGGLE FOR EQUALITY IN EGYPT: NOW A STRUGGLE FOR SURVIVAL

Vickie Janson

The struggle faced today by Coptic Christians for basic human rights and recognition as equal citizens is neither new nor, sad to say, unique to Egypt. With the rise of the Muslim Brotherhood in Egypt, however, Coptic Christians have become particularly vulnerable. Violent crimes against the Copts are increasing, though to view these incidents as localised and isolated would be wrong. Such crimes are surging all around the world and must be seen within their broader context.

The rise of the Muslim Brotherhood is, of course, the rise of political Islam, and the rise of political Islam is the rise of sharia—the rise of Islamic law. This is bad news for anyone who cares about equality and human rights. A 2011 survey undertaken in the United States of 100 random mosques illustrates this point well, and highlights that there is nothing localised about the problem of theologically sanctioned violent crime against non-Muslims. The survey was conducted to measure the correlation between sharia adherence and dogma calling for violence against nonbelievers. And the results are telling:

Mosques that presented as Sharia adherent were more likely to feature violence-positive texts on site than were their non-Sharia-adherent counterparts. In 84.5% of the mosques, the imam recommended studying violence-positive texts. The leadership at Sharia-adherent mosques was more likely to recommend that a worshipper study violence-positive texts than leadership at non-Sharia adherent mosques. Fifty-eight percent of the mosques invited guest imams known to promote violent jihad. The leadership of mosques that featured violence-positive literature was more likely to invite guest imams who were known to promote violent jihad than was the leadership of mosques that did not feature violence-positive literature on mosque premises.[31]

So in mosques where sharia compliance is promoted—a feature of political Islam—there is an increase in the promotion of violence against non-Muslims *and* an escalation in human rights abuses generally. Sharia adherence causes problems. The rise of the Muslim Brotherhood and political Islam in Egypt shows what happens when this theology is applied to a society.

In Egypt, churches and Christians have been attacked, and Coptic girls have been abducted, raped, forcibly converted to Islam, and married against their will to Muslim men. Why? Because according to sharia, Christians are inferior to Muslims. While Coptic Christians are familiar with systematic discrimination, this greater emphasis on sharia compliance under an Islamist regime merely legalises the continuing inequality. Minorities are suffering. And no one is suffering more than the minority within the minority: Egypt's Christian women. Islamic sharia devastates women's rights and autonomy.

But sharia wrath in Egypt is not limited to Copts, with mainstream Egyptian television covering (earlier 2012) the slow beheading of a Tunisian Muslim convert to Christianity—a sharia punishment for apostates. Although much of the worldwide Muslim community displays zero tolerance for any publicity they deem offensive, it is ironic that a person can be beheaded on mainstream Egyptian television. No one rioted for this poor soul's treatment; no one declared this an offence against humanity and decency.

In another display of growing extremism, even contemporary celebrations are being hijacked for Islamist purposes. In March 2012, for instance, the Egyptian Parliament recognised International Women's Day. Yet the Parliament chose to celebrate the day by calling for less human rights for women, even though earlier in the year there had been a degree of outrage when woman were subjected to virginity testing. In calling for less human rights for women, the Egyptian

---

Parliament condemned the 1978 UN convention against gender discrimination as being "incompatible with the values of Islamic sharia".

Egypt's new draft constitution is also more sharia compliant. This is hardly surprising given that the spiritual leader of the Muslim Brotherhood, Dr Yusuf al-Qaradawi, assisted in its drafting. This is a man who only two years ago publicly stated that Muslims must obey the commands of Islam's prophet—even to murder. The clear prohibitions against slavery in the former Egyptian constitution have been removed, since slavery is a sharia-approved Islamic principle. The new draft includes neither a clear ban on human trafficking nor an obligation to adhere to international rights treaties. This is terrible for Egypt's Christian minority—especially the many young Christian girls who are abducted, raped, and forced to convert to Islam.

Yet all girls will suffer, not just Christians.

In line with the sharia dictate allowing girls as young as nine years to be wed, the newly drafted constitution provides no minimum age limit for marriage. This will only fuel the child-bride and sex-slave industries, and is deeply worrying for all Egypt's daughters, especially in light of a 2011 report detailing gender- and religious-based violence against Coptic women and girls in particular. To quote from this report, "Tell My Mother I Miss Her" by Michele Clark and Nadia Ghaly:

> Coptic women in Egypt are disappearing from their homes, their schools, and their places of work. They go missing while returning from church, picking up their children from school, or traveling to the sick bed of an aging parent. They are often held as captives, subjected to physical and psychological abuse in the form of rapes, beatings, domestic labor without pay, forced marriage and forced conversion to Islam. Their lives, and the lives of their families, are severely damaged.

This is a tragedy. Rather than a progressive move into a liberal form of democracy, many Copts fear a regression to an even stricter prejudicial legal framework than the one introduced after the coup in 1952. There are even rumblings that resemble the declarations of early leaders, like Fatimid Caliph al-Hakem B'Amr Allah (996–1021). He decreed that any person, including women and children, using the Coptic language in the home or street would be punished by cutting his tongue. Consequently, the Coptic Patriarch Gabriel II (1131–1145) declared that all liturgical readings take place in Arabic.[32]

We would all expect cutting out a person's tongue to be relegated to the dark ages. Yet Dr Abdullah Badr, an Al-Azhar graduate and a professor of Islamic exegesis, recently announced the return of this age of intolerance. He threatened that those who mock sharia or Islam would have their tongues cut out.

This worldwide trend to stop all criticism of Islam takes a less-violent form in Western nations, where they use "lawfare" rather than warfare. Yet it produces a similar result: it silences all opposition and legally cuts out the tongues of critics. As in Egypt, however, there will always be some sharia zealots spurred on by the decree to wield the sword of Islam and physically remove freedom of speech: the foundation stone of liberal democracy and the thorn in the side of Islamists.

The rise of the Muslim Brotherhood has also allowed political Islam to flourish—along with draconian sharia laws and punishments. What was once the Coptic struggle for equality appears now to have regressed to a struggle for survival.

~~~~~~

Vickie Janson is the Victorian Senate candidate for the federal political party Australian Christians <http://www.australianchristians.com.au>. She is also the author of Ideological Jihad, which outlines the struggle of ideas in understanding Islam in Australia. Vickie is a public speaker and a human rights advocate who resides in Melbourne with her husband, Michael, and her son.

---

[32] See Iris Habib El-Misry, *The Story of the Coptic Church*, book 3 (Arabic), p. 134.

9. THE FORCED CONVERSION OF COPTIC WOMEN

Nadia Ghaly

Egypt is home to the indigenous Coptic Christian community, the largest non-Muslim group in the Middle East. But the religious freedom of Egypt's eight-million-strong Coptic Christian community is threatened by terrorism from extreme Islamic groups, by the abusive practices of local police forces, and by discriminatory Egyptian Government policies.

Reports produced by different groups, including Christian Solidarity International, detail many of the problems faced by Coptic Christians in Egypt. Although Muslims and the Egyptian Government dispute reports of forced conversions of Coptic women and girls to Islam by Muslim men, there are credible reports of kidnappings and forced conversions that cannot be disputed. And, on 23 March 2004, the late Coptic Pope Shenouda III publicly condemned the kidnappings and forced conversions of Christian girls—who are often lured, by Muslim men, into running away from their homes.

The following cases are just a handful of the many reported abductions being investigated.[33]

---

[33] For more details, see "Tell my mother I miss her: the disappearance, forced conversions and forced marriages of Coptic Christian women in Egypt (II)", a report written by Michele Clark and Nadia Ghaly for Christian Solidarity International. This report, which was accessed on 9 December 2012, can be found online at <http://www.scribd.com/doc/101549890/Tell-My-Mother-I-Miss-Her>.

Case one

Date of disappearance: 28 August 2011

Victim: Amal, a 17-year-old girl

Summary: On 11 August 2011, the victim's father received a threatening call. The caller said the following: "Take care of your daughter." The number appeared on the father's screen. He tried to call back and send texts, but received no answer. He reported the threats to the police, but received no response.

For almost two weeks, the father stayed at home to take care of his daughter; finally, however, he had to go to work. He was gone for a few hours and when he returned, his daughter was gone. She had asked her mother for permission to go to the supermarket, 250 meters from her house. She was bored, and she complained about being locked up. She had been gone for 15 minutes.

Her father went after her but could not find her. He looked everywhere and could find no signs of her. He reported the disappearance to the police, who sent him from one station to the other. Although he was finally able to file a report, his complaint was not taken seriously. He asked that the phone number be traced; it was sent to the investigation department, and he was told that this could take three weeks. He conducted his own research and was able to get a name, but the police did nothing to follow up. The parents have heard nothing from their daughter since her disappearance.

Since that time, the father learned of four similar cases of unexplained and unreported disappearances of daughters in his neighbourhood. He placed missing-persons advertisements in the newspapers but received no response. The mother remains distraught, and the father writes anguished poems about his daughter.

Case two

Date of disappearance: 20 May 2011

Victim: Mary, a 19-year-old single woman living at home

Summary: The victim is a 19-year-old girl who had finished her training as a computer technician. She had not returned home from work. Her mother reported her absence to the police at 6:00 PM, yet there was no formal accusation. At 11:00 PM the police came to the home and told the family that the victim had married a Muslim man. The mother had a stroke, and the rest of the family thought she had left willingly with her new husband.

On 20 June 2011, the victim was moved from Cairo to another city, from where she called her father. The father recorded this initial conversation, which is abruptly interrupted by the sound of a man entering the room. In a subsequent call, the man said, "She is unconscious now, but let me tell you something: this girl is more important to me than anything else. I swear to God if something happens to her, I will kill all of you—and I will burn the church. And you know that I can do that."

The victim's lawyer took the case to the Attorney General and requested three things: first, address the threats to the father and the church in the recorded message; second, allow the father to meet with his daughter; and, third, respect the daughter's wishes with regard to her religious identity. To date, the lawyer has received no response.

The victim has now called her father eight times, asking for some kind of help. She speaks to him of abuse and mistreatment.

She is with Muslims and reports that she is beaten when she makes the sign of the cross. She is imprisoned in a room and occasionally has access to a phone. The father knows where she is but is afraid that if he tries to intervene, the consequences will be worse. His position in the army does not help. Out of desperation, the father told her to cut herself so that her new Muslim family would take her to the hospital; there, he might get a chance to see her. Unfortunately for him, her Muslim family asked the doctor to dress her wounds at their house.

Case three

Date of disappearance: 30 June 2010

Victim: Mary-Anne, a married woman with three children under 18 years of age

Current status: The victim and her children remain missing. The victim's mother has had no personal contact with them and learned about their conversion on a YouTube video.

Summary: On 30 June 2010, the victim's mother was admitted to a hospital. Her married daughter, who lived in another city, was planning to come and care for her. When she did not show up, the mother began to worry and called the victim's husband, who said his wife had left as planned. The victim's mother reported the disappearance to the police, who reluctantly registered the disappearance of the young woman and her three children. With no support from the authorities, the victim's mother spent considerable personal resources trying to uncover clues about her family's whereabouts. She learned that her daughter had befriended a Muslim woman in her neighbourhood, who also vanished on the same day, and that her granddaughter had a close male Muslim friend at the university. She subsequently learned that her granddaughter married this man.

Case four

Date of disappearance: 14 June 2007
Victim: Waffa, a 19-year-old single woman
Source of information: Personal interviews with the mother and the family's lawyer
Current status: The mother has seen her daughter one time since her abduction.
Summary: The victim went to meet friends for pizza and never came home. Her friends said she was not feeling well and left the gathering early with a Muslim girl. The police reluctantly filed a report. The family has had minimal contact with her, and the mother has seen her only once since her abduction. Although the father learned she was forced to marry a Muslim, the mother has heard reports the daughter is being blackmailed with accusations of prostitution and that she feels trapped. The victim's family launched an appeal on television stating that they loved her and wanted her back—but they have received no results.

Case five[34]

Date of disappearance: 30 September 2012
Victim: Sarah Ishaq Abdelmalek, a 14-year-old girl
Summary: The victim was going to school when she disappeared. Her abduction happened in a little village called El Dabaa, near Mersa Matrouh, where the Salafis have a strong presence. Her father filed a report with the police, who informed him that his daughter had

---

[34] For more information about this case, see the following report written by Mary Abdelmassih on 2 November 2012 for AINA: <http://www.copts.co.uk/index.php?option=com_content&task=view&id=4297&Item id=1>. This article was accessed on 9 December 2012.

converted to Islam and married a Salafi (an extreme Muslim). However, Egypt's law states that the minimum age for marriage or conversion to another religion is 18 years. The Islamists are now refusing to return the teenager to her family, insisting she is 18 years of age rather than 14. Although the victim's father produced a birth certificate showing the girl to be 14 years of age, the authorities have refused to act.

The Coptic Church, the victim's family, and its legal representation approached the Egyptian President Mohamed Morsi. Yet they received no help from the State. Human rights organisations, including the National Council of Women, also lobbied for the victim to be returned to her family. In response, the Salafist Front released the following statement on 28 October 2012:

> Attempts [by] the church and human rights organisations to put pressure on the Interior Ministry to return the girl is rejected in form and substance, confirming that the girl has full freedom to convert to Islam and [has] full freedom to marry as long as "she has reached puberty and can withstand marriage with its consequences and responsibilities". We will address, in any way, attempts to force Sarah to do anything against her freedom.

From all these cases, a pattern emerges. The Christian girls are young, with the majority under 18 years of age. They are from rural or low socioeconomic backgrounds. They have a limited education. They are befriended by Muslim girls. And many Christian girls are even drugged.

When the girls are abducted, they are placed in *El Gamayah El Shariah*—juristic associations where veiled women teach them the Koran and force them into converting to Islam. These juristic associations were founded in 1912 by Sheikh Mahmoud Khattab Subki; today, there are more than 6,000 juristic-association centres across Egypt. They are financed by donations from Al-Azhar University, the Egyptian Government, and several Islamic countries—particularly the Kingdom of Saudi Arabia. Although these associations function under the guise of a charity—pretending to give medical, educational, and women's health advice—their real purpose is stated in their charter: juristic associations aim to invite people to adhere to the teachings of Islam, and correct misconceptions broadcast by the enemies of Islam among its citizens, through the holding of seminars and lectures held in the mosques of the Assembly. These "teachings of Islam" occur in the back of each centre, where the newly converted are kept under lock, key, and guard to ensure their captivity—while they are forced to convert to Islam.

The Coptic Christians in Egypt are not fighting only the perpetrators; they are also battling Al-Azhar University, the Egyptian Government, other Islamic governments, and strong Islamic organisations. This is what each one of these poor Coptic girls is facing. Is this a fair fight?

The status of Coptic women—and particularly minors—in post-revolutionary Egypt is a major concern. This is especially the case since the Islamist-led government has enshrined sharia law into Egypt's new constitution. So how will Egypt's Coptic women be treated under the current regime? Must Egypt's Copts accept sharia principles, even if it were to mean that they would never see their daughters again? What does sharia law say about non-Muslim women? Who will interpret such sharia laws or principles?

I will finish with what Jesus said: "Blessed are you when people insult you, persecute you, and falsely say all kinds of evil against you because of me." Are Jesus' words directed at the Coptic Christians? I wonder.

~~~~~~

Nadia Ghaly is a journalist, a librarian, a human rights activist, and a mother. She was born in Egypt but now lives in Australia. She is inspired by the words of Frederick Douglass: "Knowledge makes a man unfit to be a slave."

10. What is in a Name?

Dr Moheb Ghaly

"Martha is Christian; she will always remain so."
Of course, it came as little surprise to me that, because of this simple but clear testimony, Martha, a
medical student, was failed.

—*Ein Shams University, Cairo, Egypt, 1967*

Notable Copts, there are many—for instance, esteemed Emeritus Professor Dr Emil A Tanagho, a urologist, and Professor Sir Magdy Yacoub, a cardiothoracic surgeon knighted by Queen Elizabeth II in 1991. But what do these two Copts have in common? Both were denied the opportunity to work in Egypt—on religious grounds—and both left for the United Kingdom and the United States, respectively, where they have achieved international recognition for their work. Perhaps one exception to this is the Egyptian urologist and Egyptologist Wassim Al-Sissy. Unlike many doctors who have left Egypt, he advocates for Copts in situ.

There are, of course, many other renowned Copts in various fields. For example, Boutros Boutros-Ghali, the famous Egyptian politician and diplomat, was the sixth Secretary-General of the United Nations during the 1990s. And, closer to home, Nick Kaldas, APM, holds the position of Deputy Commissioner of the NSW Police.

What is common in these cases, and also in my own, is the *flourishing* that happens upon leaving Egypt. The act of leaving triggers this flourishing. It seems a great shame that to flourish one has to leave Egypt and seek a better life in the West. But this opportunity is reserved for those who are fortunate enough and have the means to leave in the first place. The fate that befalls those who are not given this choice cannot be overstated, particularly with the current political climate in Egypt.

In remembering my own experiences, I am struck by the systematic institutional discrimination that blights Egypt—and how that led to my journey as a doctor, starting in England and ending in Australia.

Martha

I was born in Cairo in 1950, and lived there until I was 25 years of age. I graduated from medicine in 1974 and worked in Egypt for two years, before leaving for England to work and continue my training. I obtained the Fellowship of the Royal College of Surgeons (FRCS) four years later. After returning to Egypt in 1979, knowing the Egyptian Army would be looking for me, I completed the compulsory army service and arrived in Australia with my wife, Mona, in February 1981.

Discrimination occurred in the Egyptian education system. First, there were more opportunities for Muslim students to enrol in their own university, Al-Azhar University, where Christians were forbidden. During my studies at Ein Shams University in Cairo, I witnessed discrimination against Christians, especially in oral and clinical exams. I recall a student by the name of Boulos Boulos, who was told by the professor conducting the oral examination, "I usually fail one Boulos. And you, well, you are two!" He ushered him out of the room without examining him and then failed him. This is just one example of the blatant institutional discrimination resulting from the name "Boulos", or "Paul" in English, which is a Christian name.

Later, when I was working in England and preparing for the final examinations, I bumped into the same Dr Boulos Boulos while he was lecturing at the Royal Free Hospital in London. I was reminded of the discrimination he faced in his own country many years earlier and compared it with his achievements in this new country.

I also recall the story of a student named Martha. When an examiner mockingly asked her, "Martha, is that name Christian or Muslim?" she replied, "Martha is Christian; she will always remain so." After I reviewed the examination results on the board, I noticed that Martha had passed all her subjects with high grades—but failed the subject involving the oral examiner who mocked her religion. So moved was I by her brave testimony, we named our first child Martha.

It is a common custom for Coptic Christians to be identified by their name or a cross tattooed on the wrist. Because I lack a tattoo and my name is neutral, neither Muslim nor Christian, a lecturer infamous for failing Christians did not know how to categorise me. I recall, in an oral examination, this examiner asking me to show him the structures on the front of the wrist—and, naturally, he insisted I show him my right wrist. Looking for the cross tattoo, while I presented the structures of the wrist, and finding nothing, I assume he resolved that I was Muslim. And that is why I passed and received a distinction.

This shows that institutional discrimination can be overt or subtle. Although this institutional discrimination occurred in the 1960s, today there is not even a question of name origins. It is visual; female Christian students are unveiled. Recently, I read in a newsletter about the charity Coptic Orphans. This charity described a Christian girl too terrified to attend school—even fully veiled. She has to brave the bullying at her school and is mistreated, because she is Christian.

Returning

In the 1970s and 1980s, Christians left Egypt to improve their standard of living and to avoid more discrimination; now, they are leaving because they fear for their safety and are terrified of losing their lives. We hear of kidnappings, killings, and attacks on properties and Coptic Churches all over the country. Neither justice nor security exists.

I have returned to Egypt twice, primarily to do some volunteer work and to accompany my daughters so they could experience their cultural background. During these trips, I saw extreme poverty, lack of infrastructure—and even worse institutional discrimination against Christians in the hospital setting than in the past. Copts study and work hard, but are not offered jobs because of their religion.

Talk on the streets

My experience suggests that mainstream Australians are unaware of the suffering of minority religious groups around the world, such as the Copts in Egypt. Take Taree, Australia. It is a predominantly secular community in my experience, and only a few people show interest in overseas religious conflicts. So human rights issues for Egypt's Copts are not at the forefront.

Although the media coverage of the Arab Spring sparked some interest, even then it was clear most people were quite unaware of the complexity, context, and consequences of the situation. The Australian public was also unaware of the concern and scepticism that the Copts expressed in the wake of the Arab Spring. Many Copts understand the events of recent years must be viewed in the context of centuries of violence, martyrdom, and persecution against Coptic Christians. Reverend Dr Mark Durie describes this in his book, *The Third Choice*, which explains the Islamic concept of *dhimmitude* and what it means for non-Muslims, especially Jews and Christians. Without grasping this concept, mainstream Australia will be inflicted with the same short-sightedness as the mainstream media.

The discrimination against Martha in the late 1960s because of her name is a mild example, by today's standards, of the daily suffering experienced by Coptic Christians living in Egypt.

Working and living in a small Australian country town gives me an opportunity to represent Copts positively and to educate the public about the human rights of Egypt's Christians. I am proud to be Egyptian—but even prouder to be Australian.

I share the feelings of many Copts in the diaspora, who fear for the fate of Egypt's Copts in the wake of the Arab Spring. The Australian Coptic Movement Association's efforts and commitment to Coptic Christians in Egypt is commendable.

~~~~~~

Dr Moheb Ghaly is a specialist general surgeon who has been practising for 27 years in Taree, Australia. In 2012, he was awarded an Order of Australia Medal for his services to medicine and the community. He is a proud Australian and Coptic Christian.

11. BUILDING A NEW PYRAMID FOR EGYPT

Nermien Riad

The Pyramids of Giza represent the cornerstone of Egyptian pride. If you attend any gathering of Copts, you will hear at least one person appeal to the Pyramids as proof that Egyptians can do great things—if they work together.

But do Copts in the diaspora understand they have the potential to pull off an accomplishment on the scale of the Pyramids once again? Do Copts realise that a project as huge as the Pyramids has already begun, and that they, too, can become a part of it?

Coptic Orphans, an international development organisation founded in 1988, has started something big in Egypt. Through child sponsorship and a network of hundreds of village-based volunteers supported by local churches and organisations, our programs help fatherless children stay in school and reach their full potential.

In 2011, Coptic Orphans, in collaboration with the US-based George Washington University, commissioned the first large-scale survey of the Coptic diaspora in major English-speaking lands of immigration: Canada, Australia, the United States, and the United Kingdom. The results reveal that Copts enjoy many resources, which can be used to help Egypt.

Coptic Orphans has tapped some of these resources, and created a three-tier model based on the work of *individuals*, *small groups of Copts*, and *the diaspora at large*. Such cooperation is helping to build a new

Great Pyramid in Egypt, consisting of social and educational development.

This is a wonder of human flourishing—the best pyramid Egyptians can construct today.

Individuals

Here is an impressive fact about the Great Pyramid (the largest of the three Pyramids in the Giza Necropolis): it is constructed from 2.3 million *individual* blocks.

Estimates vary on just how many Copts live outside Egypt, but most suggest there are between 150,000 and 1.5 million Copts in the diaspora. Just as the Great Pyramid started with individual stones, however, there is no way to avoid the hard work of building thousands—or millions—of individual links, person by person, from the diaspora to the homeland.

The Coptic diaspora survey indicates that 92 per cent of Copts have made donations to Egypt during the last three years, with an average of $7,310 donated per person in 2011.[35]

Ninety-five per cent of respondents said that the future of Egypt is important to them.[36] Yet we find that the ones who translate their interest into action are those who make a real-life connection to Egypt.

Child sponsorship became our answer to the real-life connection. Sponsors could support educational and development programs in Egypt, and have the privilege of maintaining a personal commitment to a child's progress in those programs through correspondence and visits.

Today, Coptic Orphans has more than 4,000 sponsored children in its programs. Each individual relationship between a Copt outside Egypt and a child inside Egypt is an individual block in a growing structure that supports our brothers and sisters in Egypt.

Although 35 per cent of Copts surveyed said they volunteered their time and resources for Egypt while remaining in their country of residence, a full 57 per cent said they would like to volunteer their time

---

[35] Brinkerhoff, JM & Riddle, L 2012, "General findings: Coptic diaspora survey", Elliott School of International Affairs of George Washington University in collaboration with Coptic Orphans, p. 14. This report can be downloaded from <http://www.copticorphans.org/sites/all/uploads/reports/CopticSurveyReport2-2012.pdf>. A copy was downloaded on 5 December 2012.

[36] ibid., p.11.

and resources if possible. Likewise, 10 per cent said they went to Egypt to volunteer, whereas 25 per cent said they would like to go to Egypt and volunteer if they could.[37]

It is hard to form organised and effective associations like Coptic Orphans. But when individuals become part of a larger group, they do far more good than they could have done alone.

Small groups of Copts

The Coptic diaspora survey revealed that 80 per cent of Copts outside Egypt would like to contribute to Egypt's social development more than to its political or economic growth, so informal volunteer groups have been a particularly important target for Coptic Orphans.[38]

For example, Coptic Orphans formed a program that has sent groups of 130 volunteers from six nations to Egypt. All the returning volunteers became ambassadors in their churches and diaspora associations, and at the same time enhanced the lives of 5,045 Egyptian children, to whom they taught English.

Informal groups tend to inspire other groups when they return to their countries of residence. A young Coptic American woman named Miranda Abadir came with a Coptic Orphans group to teach English to children during the summer of 2007. The next year, she brought 12 more university students back with her to build an education centre in rural Egypt. We saw the same ripple effect with other volunteers, who formed other groups and brought them to Egypt—again and again.

Many groups would also like to address the root causes of poverty. Forty-five per cent of those who responded in the Coptic diaspora survey said, instead of fulfilling basic needs, they want to "empower individuals to solve problems and become independent".[39]

It takes an organised effort to create that kind of effect in Egypt, whether by investing in education, infrastructure, and vocational training, or by providing new opportunities.

So who should lead the way among Copts?

Among all the groups in which the diaspora's Copts are active as volunteers—including the Coptic Medical Society, the Coptic Lawyers

[37] ibid., pp. 13–14.

[38] ibid., p. 11.

[39] ibid., p. 13.

Association, Coptic Orphans, Coptic World, Coptic student groups, and others—the one where Copts are most active is in the Coptic Orthodox Church.

The Coptic Church is the source of Coptic identity as a distinct group in Egypt. Indeed, one could argue that all service in the Coptic community flows from the Eucharist, the heart of the Coptic Liturgy.

Eight-two per cent of Copts, who responded to the survey, included their Church among the organisations and groups through which they bless the Egyptian homeland. And 72 per cent said the Church was the one organisation in which they were most active.[40]

Even more than those who are active, 87 per cent of Copts prefer to give through their local church.[41] What would happen if Coptic congregations outside Egypt got involved as entire churches? Churches could partner with projects and organisations in Egypt who have the expertise to address the root cause of poverty. Church volunteers could form groups and go to Egypt to help those in need.

The diaspora at large

This leads to the pinnacle of diaspora achievement. By adding value to the Coptic diaspora at large, Copts can strengthen some of their more important institutions, such as prominent dioceses in the diaspora. Copts can also draw the attention of others, such as legislators in their home nations.

Here is an example. His Grace Bishop Angaelos, General Bishop of the Coptic Orthodox Church in the United Kingdom, is well known for his ministries among the youth, and he is highly sought after for his subtle and complex analyses of social, political, and religious realities that influence the global Coptic Orthodox Church. On 19 September 2012, His Grace spoke to numerous parties in the US Government— including Library of Congress scholars, the US State Department, the US Commission on International Religious Freedom, and others— about the Copts in Egypt. A small handful of congressional representatives, including the Office of Gus Bilirakis, a Republican representing Florida's Twelfth Congressional District, also became a part of the event.

---

[40] ibid., p. 12.

[41] ibid., p. 15.

This was only possible because thousands of Copts had come together to form and maintain organisations like Coptic Orphans, which supported and helped coordinate the visit. Through Coptic Orphans as an organised group, Copts reached key voices outside the Coptic community about the situation in Egypt.

The Coptic diaspora survey also gives leaders and institutions within the Coptic diaspora valuable information about how people remain connected to Egypt, how much they donate to Egypt, and how their Egyptian identity meshes with the one developed in their home country. By learning more about the dynamics of our diaspora and making it available to the international development and political spheres, Coptic Orphans is helping legislators and donors learn about the Coptic diaspora's potential to improve Egypt.

So the diaspora rests upon a foundation based on the individual and then the group. The diaspora unites the three into one.

The growing movement among Copts has the potential to do great things. Will the Coptic diaspora rise and build the next great wonder of the world in Egypt?

~~~~~~

Nermien Riad founded Coptic Orphans in 1988, after volunteering for an orphanage in Cairo. When she saw that most of the children had living widowed mothers who could not afford to feed them, she gathered family and friends to sponsor children in Egypt. Today, Coptic Orphans works through a network of 400-plus church-based volunteers in Egypt, who visit fatherless families in their homes and make sure they receive everything they need to unlock the children's full potential. That way, they do not have to get married off as child brides, work as 10-year-old family breadwinners, or go live in an institutional orphanage. For more information about Coptic Orphans, please visit <http://www.copticorphans.org>.

12. What to Tell Them

Luke Girgis

The Lord proclaims his goal and plan for humanity when he teaches us to pray for "earth as it is in heaven" (Matthew 6:10). What does this mean? Well, it means exactly what it says. Our Creator aims to achieve a reality on Earth that is exactly like the reality in heaven. This is illustrated quite clearly in the opening verses of Revelation 21, where John paints for us an image reminiscent of the Garden of Eden, pointing towards God's inevitable victory over all evil:

> Now I saw a new heaven and a new earth. … And I heard a loud voice from heaven saying, "Behold, the tabernacle of God is with men, and He will dwell with them, and they shall be His people. God Himself will be with them and be their God." … Then He who sat on the throne said, "Behold, I make all things new."

John's revelation reveals that eventually God will conquer all. He will achieve His goal of a new heaven and a new Earth, and we will welcome Him to dwell amongst us again. Importantly, we notice that in Revelation 21 it describes a nature that is not entirely foreign to the one we find currently on Earth. We see that there is a heaven and an Earth—but with the key difference being that "all things" have been made "new". So, essentially, we are fighting for the planet that we are currently living on. And, as Christians, we can choose to either align ourselves with the Lord's side to achieve a renewed creation—or rebel against it.

CS Lewis points out that, "Christianity, if false, is of no importance, and if true, [is] of infinite importance. The only thing it cannot be is moderately important." This, I think, highlights the significance of what Saint Paul tells us in 2 Corinthians 5:17, when he says, "If anyone is in Christ, the new creation has come." Plainly, if we want to be part of the Lord's new creation, here and now, then we must live in Christ fully. If we truly believe in Christianity, then lukewarmness in any aspect of our lives is not an option. And as we learn from Revelation 3:16, Jesus will spit the lukewarm out. So, as Christians, our faith—that is, our goal to be part of the new creation, here and now—should be our highest, and arguably our only, priority.

The most shameful realisation for me is that even as an average income earner, living comfortably in the West, my seemingly "proactive" steps to join the Lord in His battle for the renewing of creation may, in reality, be extremely superficial. This is something I pray about constantly, for there is nothing more I want than to live on an Earth that is at ultimate peace with itself—where humans not only love one another but also love their Creator and the creation that was made for them.

When we shift our eyes to Egypt, we see the battle being lost on all fronts—for now. And, as a Christian, it is obvious that doing nothing of significance is essentially fighting against the Lord and His plan. Doing nothing is surrendering and letting the enemy take reign; no war has ever been won through inaction.

This struggle spurred me to write the song and prayer "What to Tell Them". I am a Sydney-based Christian musician whose fan base is predominantly secular—yet, ironically, I go by the stage name of Coptic Soldier. The lyrics below were written to illustrate to my listeners the current reality in Egypt and to call for an end to the hypocritical way in which we respond to the situation. I find this hypocrisy residing within me. But I also see it in Egyptians throughout the West, who choose to ignore the hells in our homeland because of various work and social commitments.

Coptic Christians oh so nervous
Christmas bullets, they spray church front
No one knows that the homeland's hurting
She screams so loud but no man's heard her

Military tanks run over the children
And anyone that is at a protest for Christians
I was asked in an interview if I was put in their position
Could I ever forgive them? But

I don't know what to tell them
I don't know what to tell them
I hope that I could, Lord knows that I should but

I don't know what to tell them
I don't know what to tell them
We don't know that minute until we are in it

I sponsor an orphan in Egypt
But when I was there I had no time to see him
Come to think of it
In five years I've only written ever one letter, that's greedy

He wrote back and said his mumma got sick
And because he loved God daddy couldn't get jobs
And he hates school 'cause he's so different
Then asked if I would pay him a visit?

I don't know what to tell him
I don't know what to tell him
I'd say that I'd visit, can't believe that I didn't
I don't know what to tell him

I don't know what to tell him
We don't know that minute until we are in it
I've seen a picture of Muslims shielding Christians as they pray
I've seen a picture of Christians shielding Muslims as they pray

Can love conquer theology?
We know peace is found in grace
Will Egypt ever reach a democracy?
Where Christian and Muslim rights sound the same?

Arab spring? More like hell's there
and will a march in the streets of Sydney help them?
I wonder what I would tell them
If they asked me to pack your bags, go and help them

Grace is unbound

We need to keep pulling on heaven till it comes down
Brother Ali and Gungor will touch down
And sing there's no me and you, but us now.

~~~~~~

Make no mistake about it: the Lord is at war and we shall all choose our side, whether we are conscious of the decision we make or not.

13. TRIBUTE TO HIS HOLINESS POPE SHENOUDA III

Ramy Tadros

His Holiness Pope Shenouda III of Alexandria and the Patriarch of the Coptic Orthodox Church
Born 3 August 1923 | Died 17 March 2012
Papacy Began 14 November 1971 | Papacy Ended 17 March 2012[42]

Egypt is enduring tumultuous times: revolutions, economic collapse, escalating attacks against the Coptic Christians—and, now, the death of His Holiness Pope Shenouda III of Alexandria and the Patriarch of the Coptic Orthodox Church. Although his death has overwhelmed all Egyptians and Coptic Christians, many other populations throughout the world have also been saddened. People throughout Africa and the Middle East have been particularly distressed at the loss of His Holiness. And, even in Australia, almost 15,000 kilometres away, 17 Federal Members of Parliament offered their condolences during parliament.

But the anguish was strongest in Egypt, where His Holiness' funeral attracted one of the largest crowds ever witnessed for a funeral. According to a few estimates, more than 100,000 people attended St Mark's Cathedral in Cairo, Egypt, to farewell their beloved pope; however, hundreds of thousands more attended the two days of

---

[42] This tribute was written originally for the Australian Coptic Movement Association and published on 22 April 2012 at <http://www.auscma.com/2012/04/22/acms-tribute-to-pope-shenouda/>. The tribute appears as it was first published.

viewing, prompting many media outlets to call it the "funeral of the century". This huge display of grief can be attributed to his numerous ministries, which touched and changed the lives of countless persons.

Teacher, preacher, poet, reformer, peacemaker—despite all these accolades, which the people bestowed on His Holiness, his favourite title was *servant*. He served all his people, especially the youth. In a famous quotation, he said, "A church without youth is a church without a future; moreover, youth without a church is youth without a future." And despite his hectic schedule, His Holiness still managed to serve his people and the youth by conducting a meeting every Wednesday night at St Mark's Cathedral in Cairo. These weekly meetings attracted thousands, and the Church blossomed under his pastoral care. Yet this achievement is even more remarkable, considering the hostility to Coptic Christians in Egypt.

His Holiness *the reformer* helped the Church flourish on every continent. At the start of his papacy, there were three dioceses and seven churches outside Egypt, including two churches in Australia. Now, there are more than 25 dioceses and 440 churches outside Egypt, including 50 churches in Australia. But His Holiness the reformer also enhanced the ministry of women within the Coptic Church and established an order for Deaconesses. Because of his reforms, female servants now teach in the Coptic Institute and the Biblical Institute, while thousands of others instruct catechism at Sunday school.

His Holiness *the poet* wrote more than 140 books about spirituality and Christianity, the majority translated into English, French, German, Italian, and other languages. Even while exiled (1981–1985) by presidential decree for protesting against the mistreatment of Copts, His Holiness used the opportunity to serve the best way he could and he wrote 16 books.

His Holiness *the preacher* received the 1978 Browning Award for the Best Christian Preacher of the Year. And because of his scriptural and theological knowledge, he was also awarded eight honorary doctoral degrees from internationally renowned universities in Europe and the United States.

His Holiness *the peacemaker* received the 2000 UNESCO-Madanjeet Singh Prize for the Promotion of Tolerance and Non-Violence. Alluding to the scriptures, he said, "There is a way you can overcome your enemy: it is by changing your enemy into a friend. We need to win friends everywhere. ... Do not be overcome by evil, but overcome evil with good. Gentleness and meekness are needed to have peace."

Although His Holiness was a peacemaker, this never prevented him from defending the rights of his people, the Coptic Christians. And on 3 September 1981 he paid the ultimate price for protesting against the maltreatment of Copts by fundamentalist Islamic groups, when the Egyptian President Anwar El-Sadat issued a presidential decree exiling His Holiness to the Monastery of St Pishoy. A month after the decree, however, one of the fundamentalist Islamic groups, which His Holiness was protesting against, assassinated President Anwar El-Sadat. Yet it took another three and a half years, and countless appeals from within and without the Coptic Orthodox Church, for the succeeding President Hosni Mubarak to release His Holiness from exile. This finally happened on 2 January 1985.

Even after being exiled, His Holiness never hesitated from defending his people. On 2 January 2000, Muslim extremist mobs massacred 21 Coptic Christians in Kosheh, a village in Upper Egypt. Yet less than a year later, a criminal court in the Sohag Governorate released without bail all 89 defendants who were charged with the massacre. His Holiness disputed the verdict and said, "We want to challenge this ruling. We don't accept it." But as the sentence could not be appealed, he embraced his belief in pacifism and said, "We revise this sentence by God."

However, some of the worst atrocities against the Coptic Christians happened during 2011—and, as usual, His Holiness publically supported his people. The following excerpt about the 2011 Maspero Massacre is taken from the "2012 Annual Report" of the United States Commission on International Religious Freedom:

On October 9, 2011, at least 26 people were killed, mostly Coptic Orthodox Christians, and more than 300 injured in downtown Cairo after armed men confronted and attacked peaceful protestors. The demonstrators, both Christians and Muslims, were marching to the Maspero state television station to protest the September 30 destruction of a church in Aswan, Upper Egypt. Egyptian state-owned media incited the violence when broadcasters urged Egyptians to go out into the streets to protect security forces from attacks by Christian protestors. Responding to the violence, Egyptian military forces used live ammunition and excessive force, including armored vehicles that deliberately crushed and killed at least 12 protestors. Dozens of suspects have been detained and interrogated. In December, a Cairo court decided to release, pending further investigations, the remaining 27 Coptic Christian detainees arrested in connection with the violence. The investigation reportedly is ongoing.

Despite his deteriorating health and the countless threats, His Holiness presided over the funerals of the 2011 Maspero Massacre victims rather than defer the duties to other bishops. Thousands of mourners attended the funerals at St Mark's Cathedral in Cairo, and the scenes were terrifying as the families tried to grasp the tragedy's enormity. This was clearly the most blatant massacre of Coptic Christians by the Egyptian State. Yet the incident was just one of many recent attacks.

His Holiness was also a vocal defender of all Christian people, of Christian unity, of Christian solidarity. In an address given during the International Week of Prayer in 1974, he said, "The whole Christian world is anxious to see the Church unite. Christian people, being fed up with divisions, are pushing their church leaders to do something about church unity, and I am sure that the Holy Spirit is inspiring us."

Perhaps this is the most important lesson that His Holiness *the teacher* wanted his children to grasp: although these are tumultuous times in Egypt and in other lands, Christians standing united have nothing to fear. And Egypt's Copts, along with the support of all Christians, are heeding this lesson and praying for a leader who will continue to shepherd his Church and community during the uncertainty.

~~~~~~

Ramy Christopher Tadros is the author of The War of the Words: Oppression, Egypt's Copts, and the State and The Writer's Manifesto: Rules for Writing with Class.

Tadros has researched and written parliamentary documents for various Australian Commonwealth Government departments. He now writes and edits nonfiction for a living, and is the director of Proton Writing Consultants Pty Ltd <http://www.writersmarke.com>, an Australian-based writing, editing, and publishing company.

Tadros also teaches writing and editing courses at Sydney Community College.

Although Tadros likes playing with words and styling suave sentences, he also enjoys politics and economics and is pursuing postgraduate research in political economy. But, come to think of it, politics and economics are still connected with word play.

PART II
~
CULTURE, WISDOM, AND THE PAST

14. THE EMERGENCE OF THE COPTIC CHURCH: AN EVANGELICAL PERSPECTIVE

The Rev. Dr Ross Clifford & The Rev. Rod Benson

The Coptic Orthodox Church has a long and honourable history. Christian associations with Egypt began with the flight of Joseph, Mary, and Jesus to the safety of the Nile region to escape Herod's edict to kill the children in and around Bethlehem (Matthew 2:13–18). Thus, Jesus experienced the rigours of refugee life, and Egypt became his temporary refuge. Some of the successors of those hospitable Egyptians might have been founders of the first Christian churches in Egypt.

Egyptians were also among those who received the gift of the Holy Spirit at Pentecost (Acts 2:1ff), and the Christian Gospel spread from Jerusalem as pilgrims and travellers returned to their home countries. A short time later, as St Luke tells the story, Philip the Evangelist encountered an Ethiopian eunuch returning from Jerusalem to his home, reading the text of Isaiah 53:7-8 in his chariot. Philip expounded the Christian meaning of the text, and sent him on his way, converted and baptised. The eunuch may well have witnessed to the Gospel of Jesus Christ in Egypt as he passed through on his way home. Later still, the Apostle Paul enlisted a valued co-worker named Apollos, described as "a native of Alexandria ... [and] a learned man, with a thorough knowledge of the Scriptures" (Acts 18:24). It is likely that Apollos was educated in Egypt. No doubt there were many other early Egyptian converts who played important roles in the evangelisation of Egypt and the known world.

Origins of Coptic Christianity

The standard tradition of the Egyptian Church holds that St Mark the Evangelist was the founder and first bishop of the church in Alexandria.[43] Although the New Testament does not mention this, the classical historian Eusebius claims that John Mark

> was the first to be sent to preach in Egypt the gospel which he had also put into writing, and was the first to establish churches in Alexandria itself. The number of men and women who were there converted at the first attempt was so great, and their asceticism was so extraordinarily philosophic, that Philo thought it right to describe their conduct and assemblies and meals and all the rest of their manner of life.[44]

It is impossible now to identify clear links between the first Christian evangelists and converts and those who formed the Coptic Orthodox Church. Nevertheless, a particularly strong Christian presence developed in Egypt.

During the first two centuries of Christian witness, there was significant diversity in doctrine, structure, and practice among the Egyptian churches. By the end of the second century, the bishop of Alexandria imposed Catholic ecclesiasticism, bringing with it a more stringent canonical and doctrinal tradition. Many Egyptian church leaders resisted the move, and this resistance was associated with the rapid growth of monasticism in the third century, which sought not only separation from worldly influences but also independence from Catholicism. Christian monasticism, first arising in Egypt, quickly spread throughout the Christian world.[45]

---

[43] Atiya, AS 1967, *History of Eastern Christianity*, University of Notre Dame Press, Notre Dame, pp. 25–28.

[44] Eusebius, *Ecclesiastical History*, 2.16, quoted in Pearson, BA & Goehring, JE 1992, eds, *The Roots of Egyptian Christianity*, Fortress Press, Philadelphia, p. 138.

[45] Griggs, CW 1991, *Early Egyptian Christianity From its Origins to 451 CE*, EJ Brill, Leiden, The Netherlands, p. 229.

The fruit of persecution and conflict

Monasticism was also a response to persecution. Waves of intense state-sponsored violence characterised the first centuries of the Christian church, and these were particularly felt in Egypt, where so many had forged an allegiance to Jesus Christ and all that implied in terms of empire loyalty, personal morality, and community association. Christianity was a profound and growing threat to power and privilege, and those most threatened sought to destroy the new faith by killing its leaders. The period of persecution against Christians unleashed by Emperor Diocletian after 284 is known as the "Era of the Martyrs". Between 311 and 312, atrocities were committed against Christians on an unprecedented scale, with some of the worst tragedies occurring in Egypt. As church historian WHC Frend observes,

> On 25 November, Bishop Peter [of Alexandria] was executed, but it was in the villages of the Thebaid that the full horror of the situation unfolded. In these years, "thousands" were killed, as Coptic peasants deserted the old gods in droves for Christianity.[46]

Many who survived fled to the hills. When Athanasius was forced to flee Alexandria in 356, he found refuge among the monasteries of Pachomius in Upper Egypt. In Jerome's day (around 390), up to 50,000 Christian monks would gather to celebrate Easter. Persecution and martyrdom failed to extinguish the spreading flame of Christianity.

Not all was praiseworthy, though. Cyril of Alexandria, who became archbishop in 412, was not described as the most Christlike of the Church Fathers. It is said that after his death, his main theological and ecclesiastical opponents in Antioch expressed a wish that a heavy stone be placed over his grave to prevent any return of his spirit to earth.[47] Cyril was, however, a capable theologian, and his teaching inspired martyrdom in the following century. Frend notes that

> with Origen and the Cappadocians, Cyril shares the distinction of molding a whole tradition of Greek Christianity whether Orthodox or Monophysite. In his native Egypt, Coptics and Alexandrians alike looked back to him as the true champion of orthodoxy.[48]

---

[46] Frend, WHC 1984, *The Rise of Christianity*, Darton, Longman & Todd, London, p. 577.

[47] ibid., p. 753.

During the fourth century, the relative prestige of the Alexandrian See was eclipsed by Constantinople, where political and economic power was also increasingly concentrated. This, along with protracted theological disputes with church leaders at Antioch and the growing significance of the monastic movement in Egypt, led the Alexandrian bishop to break with Catholicism and cast his lot with monasticism. It was only a matter of time before an independent Egyptian Christian Church became a reality.

Forging a distinctive identity

Church historian Justo L González claims that the essential Coptic identity was refined during and after the Christological controversies of the fifth century in Egypt, culminating in the debates of the Council of Chalcedon in 451.[49] There, the Western church formally resolved disputes about the two natures of Christ, but the leaders of the Eastern church, especially in Egypt and Syria, rejected what they saw as doctrinal imposition. Other factors were also involved, including discomfort at the heavy-taxing central government based at Constantinople and longstanding cultural and ethnic tensions. In addition, the Egyptian bishops present at the Council of Chalcedon insisted that, if they signed its Definition, they would face death back home. They were not exaggerating. The Council had deposed the Alexandrian Bishop Dioscorus for his leadership in the party promoting one-nature Christology at the previous Council of Ephesus in 449. Yet his successor, appointed by Emperor Marcian, was unpopular. As church historian Diarmaid MacCulloch observes,

> On Marcian's death in 457, he was left defenceless. A mob who regarded him as a traitor to Dioscorus pursued him into the baptistery of a city church, butchered him and six of his clergy, and paraded the bleeding corpses round the city: all in the name of the *mia physis* of Jesus Christ. The emperor's authority in Egypt never

---

[48] ibid. Monophysitism refers to the tradition, especially within Egyptian Christianity, which held to the view that, after the union of the divine and the human in the Incarnation, Jesus Christ had a single nature (rather than two, one human and one divine, as the Chalcedonian Definition insisted).

[49] González, JL 1984, *The Story of Christianity, Volume 1: The Early Church to the Dawn of the Reformation*, Harper Collins, San Francisco, pp. 252–262.

fully recovered from this appalling incident. … Egyptian Christianity increasingly worshipped God in the native language of Egypt, Coptic.[50]

In Egypt, the church generally maintained an emphasis on Monophysitism in contrast to Chalcedonian Christology, and the Coptic faith continued to develop a distinctive identity and form.

The rise of Islam

Tragically, the Arab conquests of the seventh century swept away much of the Christian presence in North Africa. In Egypt, Coptic Christianity survived and became the dominant Christian church, while a smaller Chalcedonian church also continued to exist. But from the seventh to the sixteenth century, Christianity was a minority faith under the sometimes repressive shadow of Islam.

The chief reason for the resilience and sustainability of the Coptic Church seems to be that Copts were, at the time, sufficiently numerous and an important part of mainstream Egyptian society. They maintained their vernacular language in liturgy, and their distinctive theology set them apart from Byzantine Christianity, with the result that their Muslim overlords generally treated them with tolerance. Eventually, Copts adopted Arabic for everyday conversation and liturgy, but the Coptic Orthodox Church became a permanent feature of Egyptian social life.[51]

The Latin Crusades, intent on reconquering the Holy Land, did not significantly affect Egyptian Christianity, but were followed by Mongol advances. In 1250, militant Islamic Mamluks seized power in Egypt, and this proved a serious setback for Coptic Christianity, as MacCulloch writes:

> Even though Coptic Christians had little sympathy either with crusading western Christians, who regarded them as heretics, or with Mongols, who favoured Nestorians heretical in Miaphysite eyes, it was now easy for Egyptian Muslims and their rulers to regard any Christian as a fifth columnist, especially when Crusaders and Mongols turned to actual invasion of Egypt during the thirteenth century. … There was a particularly terrifying sequence of anti-Christian pogroms in 1354,

---

[50] MacCulloch, D 2011, *Christianity: The First Three Thousand Years*, Penguin Books, London, p. 233.

[51] ibid., p. 277.

when churches were torn down and both Jews and Christians were forced by mobs to recite the Islamic profession of faith, or be burned to death; unlike previous outbreaks there was little refuge, since the terror extended throughout the land, not just to Cairo. Christians were forced out of most of the best land in Egypt, "exiles in their own country". ... [The survival of Coptic Christianity] over the next three centuries was through their own efforts and the stubborn maintenance of their own traditions in their monasteries, most of which could survive only in the most remote or poverty-stricken locations.[52]

Under the guidance and protection of God, the Coptic Orthodox Church emerged from this long historical process, and has continued in post-Reformation times to bear witness to its distinctive understanding of theology and liturgy in an often hostile world.

Evangelicals and Copts

Evangelical Christians, deriving their faith and practice from Protestant emphases and the biblical traditions underpinning them, today enjoy a warm coexistence with the Coptic Orthodox Church. This is especially true in Sydney, Australia, where Bishop Daniel, head of the Diocese of Sydney and affiliated regions, has worked tirelessly to encourage ecumenical fellowship and cooperation.

Several points of convergence may be identified between aspects of the early history of Coptic Christianity, as outlined above, and the history and experience of evangelical Christianity.

Both traditions are Trinitarian and place great emphasis on the Holy Scriptures as the definitive rule for Christian faith and conduct. Both emerged in the context of fundamental theological disputation and refinement, the legacies of which remain apparent today. Both traditions grew to prominence amid persecution, although the Coptic experience of Islamic persecution, tragically repeated in Egypt today notwithstanding the so-called democratic reforms of the Arab Spring, has not yet been the experience of evangelical Christians in the West. Both also face hostility from rampant secularism and the New Atheism—not necessarily existential threats but concerted efforts to erode fundamental rights to religious freedom, freedom of conscience, and freedom of speech, on which Copts and evangelicals alike rely for the authentic practice of their faith.

---

[52] ibid., p. 278.

It is vital that all those who confess Jesus Christ as Lord seek to strengthen the bonds of fellowship that already exist among Christians, defend and promote religious freedom, work together on common causes, commend the Christian vision of reality to others, and pray earnestly for a fuller experience of the faith, hope, and love that lie at the heart of the Christian Gospel.

~~~~~~

The Reverend Dr Ross Clifford, AM, is President of the Asia Pacific Baptist Federation, Past President of the Baptist Union of Australia, President of the NSW Council of Churches, and Principal of Morling College, the Baptist Theological College in Sydney, Australia.

The Reverend Rod Benson is Public Affairs Director of the NSW Council of Churches and Ethicist and Public Theologian at Morling College.

15. A PROPOSAL FOR THE REVIVAL OF COPTIC

Emile NG Joseph

Most ethnic groups today boast their own language, in which they not only worship God, but also sing songs, tell stories, read literature, conduct business, and communicate with friends and family. Yet the Copts, the indigenous ethnic community of Egypt, lack pride in their Coptic language. They barely use it as a liturgical language, let alone as a living language for everyday use. Considering how rich and beautiful this language is, it is sad that only a minute percentage of Egyptian Christians speak it.

In this essay, we shall explore the reasons for the Coptic language's disappearance from everyday life and the language's significance for national identity and for cultural and spiritual enrichment. We shall also compare the fate of Coptic with other languages that fell into disuse or threatened to do so. Finally, we shall propose solutions for a revival, complete or partial, of the Coptic language among Coptic Christians in Egypt and in the diaspora.

A brief history

It all began with the Ancient Egyptians. Roughly 6,000 years ago, they devised an elaborate writing system to record their spoken language. This hieroglyphic writing system developed into simpler scripts: first, the priestly hieratic and, then, the demotic for everyday records.

When Alexander the Great invaded Egypt in 313 BC, the educated classes started learning Greek and teaching it to their children. About 350 years later, St Mark evangelised to the Egyptians. A missionary movement was begun, which led to the establishment of a college, the Christian School of Alexandria, where Christianity's fundamentals were taught and missionaries were trained. However, they faced a dilemma: how could they make the Christian message comprehensible to the Egyptians, not all of whom understood Greek? The missionaries knew how to read Greek but not demotic. And even though the Egyptian peasants could read neither Greek nor demotic, they were able to understand the spoken language represented by the demotic script. To ensure that the word of God be preached in the same way by all the missionaries, it had to be written in a way that the missionaries could read and that the Egyptians could understand when it was read to them. This is what led the missionaries to translate the scriptures into the Egyptian tongue by writing with the Greek alphabet. To transcribe the phonemes in demotic, which did not exist in Greek, they added supplementary characters from the former. Thus, the Egyptian language began to evolve into what is now known as Coptic.

After the persecution of the Copts under Diocletian in the early fourth century, the monastic movement started to flourish, and the Egyptian monks embraced the Coptic language to express their deep love of God and to build their communities. Then, during the life of St Shenouda the Archimandrite (348–466), the Coptic language blossomed, as it was transformed from a tool of translation or instruction into an exquisite form of expression, and reached a literary height never achieved before or equalled since.[53]

What happened to the Coptic language?

When Muslim invaders conquered Egypt during the seventh century, they coerced the Copts into learning Arabic in order to keep their government positions. This political pressure eroded the use of the Coptic language by laymen and their families. As a result, over time they even neglected to educate their children in literary Coptic. It was

---

[53] Takla, HN 1996, "The History of the Coptic Language", <http://www.stshenouda.com/coptlang/copthist.htm>, accessed 10 December 2012.

not long before Arabic loanwords crept into the Coptic language, even though Coptic was preserved in almost pure form in the Church.

However, when Hakem-bi-Amr-Allah rose to power in Egypt towards the end of the eleventh century, he persecuted the Christians, closed their churches for two-year periods, and prohibited the people from using the Coptic language. Although this period was short, it harmed the language.[54]

This was also the period when the European Crusades began. The Muslims in Egypt saw the sign of the Cross displayed on the Crusaders' armoury and inferred that they were on the side of the Copts (although the Europeans considered the Copts to be heretics). So persecutions and oppressions against them increased.

Patriarch Gabriel Ibn Turaik, in an attempt to make peace with the Muslims and show them the Copts were different from the Crusaders, introduced the use of Arabic in churches. Although this conciliatory move seemed wise at the time, it allowed Arabic into Christian literature and liturgical books, restricting Coptic to hymns and prayers. Consequently, Coptic literary use declined, and the Church and language weakened. As Coptic—which once formed a barrier to Muslim culture—declined, it was easier for more Christians to be influenced by and convert to Islam.[55]

This sorry situation continued for roughly another 500 years, until Pope Cyril IV, Patriarch of Alexandria in the nineteenth century, started a church-sponsored movement to revive Coptic by educating the clergy and introducing the Coptic language to all the schools. During this period, the Church also produced a comprehensive Coptic dictionary and several works focussing on Coptic grammar. Despite the movement continuing into the early twentieth century, the question of pronunciation and dialect eventually hindered its progress. Some Copts wished to adopt the pronunciation of modern Greek (which had been affected by years of Ottoman rule), whereas others desired to preserve the original Bohairic pronunciation (restored by scholars through extensive phonological study). This question was never resolved before the 1952 revolution, when Arabic regained its prominence. Once the Copts resumed using Arabic in their sermons, the revival process

---

[54] ibid.

[55] ibid.

weakened even more.[56] Today, there are only 300 people in the world who can speak fluent Coptic.[57]

Language and identity

The Coptic language acts as a collective identity for Copts, a people who have emerged triumphant from the furnace of countless persecutions. The language bridges the Copts with their Ancient Egyptian roots and provides them with a continuous written record of a civilisation spanning 6,000 years—the longest in history.[58]

Titti Abdel AlMessih, the only housewife who speaks Coptic fluently, says that Coptic should not be limited to religious use, or seen only as a religious relic. It is important for her, as it is to others, that the Copts figure out a way to revive their language for daily use alongside Arabic, as various minority groups in Iraq do with Kurdish or Aramaic. If the Copts fail to revive their language, then their culture and identity—the ancient Egyptian identity—might become extinct.[59] If the process of Arabisation in the Coptic Church "is not wisely put in check and eventually reversed, we are liable to face in the future a Church with a lost identity."[60]

The German philosopher Johann Gottftried von Herder supports the notion that identity and language are inextricably linked, when he says,

> Has a people anything dearer than the speech of its fathers? In its speech resides its whole thought-domain, its tradition, history, religion and basis of life, all its heart and soul. ... The best culture of a people cannot be expressed through the medium of a foreign language. ... [I]t thrives only by means of the nation's inherited and inheritable dialect. With language is created the heart of the people.[61]

---

[56] ibid.

[57] Coptic Assembly of America, 2006, "Exclusive: An Interview with the Only Coptic Family that still Speaks the Coptic Language inside Egypt", <http://www.copticassembly.org/showart.php?main_id=838>, accessed 10 December 2012.

[58] Takla, HN 1996, "The Value of Coptic: The Ecclesiastical and Coptic Principles", <http://www.stshenouda.com/coptlang/coptval.htm>, accessed 10 December 2012.

[59] Coptic Assembly of America.

[60] Takla, "The History of the Coptic Language".

Significance of the Coptic language

Those who speak and read Coptic are able to access the hidden treasures of the Church. These treasures include the language with its calligraphic script, which was used to advance the preaching of the Gospel to the native population of Egypt; the Coptic version of the Bible, which was translated using the original Greek texts that failed to survive; the writings of the Fathers of the Church and the lives of the Saints, which are included in the *Synaxarium*; the breviary, or *Agpeya*, which consists of psalms, prayers, and readings for every hour; and, lastly, the Liturgy according to St Basil, St Gregory, or St Cyril.

Since the Liturgy, the breviary, and the *Synaxarium* readings can be repeated frequently, they can also be learned by habit and explained in Sunday School, instead of being presented constantly in the vernacular. And Copts can reject the argument against Coptic—that is, the congregation no longer understands it—because the emphasis should be placed on learning and preserving the language rather than abandoning it.[62]

Comparison of Coptic with other ancient languages

Coptic is by no means a "dead" language, since there are about 300 people in the world who can speak it at various levels of conversational fluency, instead of just reciting Coptic passages from the Liturgy. Yet these people learned the language as adults, not as children "at their mother's knee".[63] This differs from the exemplar of the Hebrew revival, because Ben Yehudah, the man who almost single-handedly worked for the revival of this ancient language, made his children speak

[61] Johann Gottfried von Herder cited in Boles, D 2012, "Johann von Herder: The Best Culture of a People Cannot Be Expressed through the Medium of a Foreign Language", <http://www.copticliterature.wordpress.com/2012/08/11>, accessed 10 December 2012.

[62] Takla, "The Value of Coptic". Boles, D 2012, "Our Beautiful and Sacred Coptic language: And the Woes of Samuel of Kalamoun upon Us", <http://www.copticliterature.wordpress.com/2012/09/09/>, accessed 10 December 2012.

[63] Dunn, MC 2012, "Aramaic vs Coptic: Language Survival vs Fossilization: Parts I, II, III", <http://www.mideasti.blogspot.com.au/2012/08/>, accessed 10 December 2012.

Hebrew as a mother tongue. Other families followed suit, and Hebrew became a living language again.[64]

Hebrew never really "died", though. Jewish religious services were written and sung in Hebrew (similar to what the Copts have done with Coptic). But due to the efforts of Ben Yehuda and the political necessity of founding the Jewish State in 1948, Hebrew was raised from the ritual second language to an active first language on a national level.[65]

Like biblical Hebrew and Latin, Coptic might have disappeared from daily use, but it is still well recorded and used for ritual purposes. These languages are not "dead"—I prefer to call them "dormant"—and they can be "revived". Hebrew did not need a "resurrection". It just required the political miracle of the diaspora establishing a national homeland, modernising Hebrew, and making it the official language of the schools, military, and civil service. Likewise, any other language that shares the historical, national, and religious importance of biblical Hebrew—for example, Latin, Sanskrit, Aramaic, or Coptic—can potentially be elevated from a mere liturgical language to a national language for daily use. It only needs action combined with a national programme and sufficient political power. But if political power is lacking, the people's will to preserve their language can be powerful.[66] For instance, a Coptic revival did take place during the reign of Pope Cyril IV of Alexandria.

In the case of Aramaic (also known as Assyrian), no national programme exists to revive it, and the Assyrians even lack a nation of their own. Their language wields little political power, and no country has adopted Aramaic as their official language. Yet, somehow, there are Assyrian communities, in pockets of Iraq, Iran, Syria, and a few other countries, where the language is still spoken in daily life. There are even jokes, songs, poems, and short stories narrated in various dialects of Neo-Aramaic. In this example, the will of the people preserved the language by passing it on from one generation to the next, despite the introduction and growth of Arabic.[67]

---

[64] ibid.

[65] Stephen Fischer cited in Boles, D 2012, "Is Coptic Dead?", <http://www.copticliterature.wordpress.com/2012/08/06>, accessed 10 December 2012.

[66] ibid.

[67] Dunn, in part II of his series on Aramaic versus Coptic, suggests that the survival

What can Copts do?

Based on this essay, and remaining as realistic as we can, we cannot stage a Coptic revolution or hope for any major power shift that will allow us to establish Coptic as Egypt's national language. We can, however, follow the example of the Assyrians who still pass their language from one generation to the next, and do not limit the language to liturgical or religious use. We can also teach the Coptic language as part of the catechism in Sunday school, so that children may learn the language of the Church and appreciate its riches in the original language instead of the local vernacular. And we can pray and work for another revival, like the nineteenth century's, to the extent that the political status quo would allow it.

But the key to preserving Coptic is the will of the people. Are we willing to learn our hereditary language and communicate with it? Are we willing to write songs, stories, poetry, and literature in Coptic? Are we willing to teach it to our children and grandchildren? If we are, we are on the way to preserving our great Coptic language for generations to come.

~~~~~~

Emile NG Joseph is a Coptic Christian who has called Australia home for nearly 40 years. He teaches English and foreign languages by profession, and lives in Sydney with his wife and two children.

---

of Aramaic may be due to geography (the people who spoke it lived in remote and mountainous areas) and the expansion of Aramaic as a lingua franca in the Middle East, whereas Coptic was spoken only in Egypt and among Muslims in urban and rural areas. This is possible, of course, but the determination and goodwill of the people are still key factors. Greek was limited to Greece after 1453 AD, but still managed to survive 400 years of Ottoman rule.

16. A BRIEF TOUR OF THE COPTIC LANGUAGE

Ounas Gerges

You may be surprised to know that the Coptic language is the same language the Ancient Egyptians spoke. Although the spoken language remains almost identical, the written form has changed significantly. *Hieroglyphic* was the first type of writing using pictures. Those same inscriptions found on temples, pyramids, obelisks, burial chambers, and other places of worship were also used to write the ancient holy books.

Hieroglyphic writing was later simplified to what is known as *hieratic*, or the writing of the priests. Official statements on papyrus were written in hieratic. Hieratic then evolved into an even simpler writing system called *demotic*.

The people adopted demotic for everyday transactions, including writing deeds, scripts, letters, and inscriptions. Finally, the writing evolved into the Coptic alphabet of 32 letters, as we know it today.

The Ancient Egyptian language, or what we now call the Coptic language, remained in use throughout the periods of the Greek, Roman, and Arab conquests. All the people, regardless of their religion, spoke the language. And Coptic was the spoken language of the government, until a decree in 799 AD prohibited its use in public and private spheres. The Fatimid Caliph Al-Hakim bi-Amr Allah (996–1021) also issued strict orders preventing Egyptians from using Coptic in homes, schools, streets, mosques, and churches. Those who disobeyed the orders were punished.

Why do invaders and colonisers deliberately try to destroy a native language? They do it to undermine a native people's sense of community, culture, and identity. Yet this strategy predates the Muslim conquest of Egypt. The Greeks also tried to Hellenise the Copts.

Despite the pressure to eradicate the Coptic language, the Copts preserved it and continued to use it in their literature, prayers, and church services. The people even kept on speaking the language right through to the fifteenth century. Although the number of people using Coptic dwindled throughout the following years, according to several reliable sources, certain parts of Upper Egypt still embraced the language until the eighteenth century. Today, several families in Egypt speak Coptic, and many others have started using the language in their homes.

Coptic has also survived as a biblical text. During the second century in Alexandria, Egypt, the Holy Bible was translated from the original Greek text into the Coptic language. This was done by scholars who were proficient and knowledgeable in the Greek and Egyptian languages. As a consequence, the Coptic translation of the Holy Bible is considered to be one of the most accurate and reliable translations available. So whenever the meaning or intent of a certain Bible verse (in English or another language) is ambiguous, scholars can examine the Coptic text to clarify the message.

Coptic language and Coptic culture

Culture includes many things: a people's art, cuisine, clothing, lifestyle, beliefs, customs, etiquette, social institutions and, most importantly, language. Transmission of culture and identity is possible only through the fundamental vehicle of language.

Language helps a population express and understand its culture. As a means of communicating values, beliefs, and customs, the Coptic language fosters feelings of group identity and solidarity. The Coptic language connects the Copts with their Ancient Egyptian ancestors and civilisation, which is more than 5,700 years old. When a language disappears, a culture dies.

The Coptic language also reveals the priceless wisdom found in Coptic-written books—for example, letters, stories, legal documents, the Bible, the Liturgy, histories of the Coptic church, histories of the Patriarchs of Alexandria, writings of the Church Fathers, lives of the Saints, and the Church canon laws.

Although many ancient texts are written in Coptic, the people still speak the language. As a result, the term "revival" is a grim-sounding word that I dislike using, because it does not apply to Coptic. Revival means the language is "dead", and a dead language is a language that lacks native speakers—people who grew up speaking the language as children.

But I, for one, spoke Coptic as a child. My brother and sisters spoke it as children, too. Coptic is our first language. Yet my cousins and their children and their children's children also speak Coptic. Even my children's first language is Coptic, whereas their second language is English.

You may call Coptic "endangered"—but certainly not dead. Hence, I would like to say, let us revitalise rather than revive the language.

Let us collectively inspire and encourage the younger generations to take pride and interest in their ancestral language. And by teaching them the language, it will allow them to read traditional Coptic literature, use it for cultural and religious purposes, and speak it as a first or second language.

Coptic-speaking people exist today, because a few families and many individuals kept using the Coptic language in their homes and with friends. But to revitalise and spread the language more effectively, more people must become enthusiastic about it and their heritage. People need to be serious about using the language as much as possible, in as many aspects of their lives as possible.

Ironically, though, the entire Egyptian population is already speaking partly in Coptic. In their everyday language, Egyptians use many words and expressions without even realising they are uttering words of Coptic and Ancient Egyptian origin. Egyptian Arabic borrows numerous Coptic words; this is why it differs from other Arabic dialects. If the Egyptian colloquial word is absent from the Arabic dictionary, it probably originates from Coptic.

Is it possible to revive Coptic?

Here is a list of revived languages: Ainu, Barnagarla, Belarusian, Chochenyo, Cornish, Hawaiian, Hebrew, Kaurna, Latin, Lazuri, Leonese, Manx, Maori, Occitan Gascon, Palawa kani (a Tasmanian language), Sanskrit, and Wampanoag. All these languages were dead before being revived.

To cite a specific example, the Welsh revitalised their Welsh language and, of all the current Welsh speakers, more than 50 per cent are under the age of 30. So it is important to concentrate on teaching the children and young people the language.

In the case of the Coptic language, revitalisation applies since people still speak it. And the families and individuals who speak Coptic in Egypt and abroad are proof that a complete revival or rejuvenation of the language is possible.

Ideas for reviving the language

Picenti Rizkalla Gerges and his Coptic-speaking family (that is, his brothers and sister and their children and their children's children) became living legends, an embodiment of the revival for others to emulate.

Gerges, from a young age, displayed great passion for Coptic. Although he spent all his life studying and researching the language, he also helped to raise awareness of its importance in conversation and literature.

Gerges taught the language everywhere he could, from schools to associations to monasteries throughout Egypt. When he saw the people's enthusiasm for Coptic, he dedicated more of his time to the cause.

To help would-be speakers and readers of Coptic, Gerges compiled a comprehensive Arabic–Coptic dictionary consisting of about 47,000 words. This was a continuation—and an expansion—of the dictionary that his father, Rizkalla Gerges, started.

Picenti Rizkalla Gerges also accumulated a list of words that have a Coptic (Ancient Egyptian) origin and are used in the Egyptian Arabic language. He wrote and published songs, poems, and stories in Coptic, and he authored and co-authored many books to help people learn the language.

I recall some of the methods Gerges, who is also my uncle, used to teach the family, particularly the children, new Coptic words or phrases. He would post signs everywhere around the house: "Speak your language, the Coptic language." The signs were designed to encourage guests, friends, and family to speak the language in the home. And I recall that whenever he would call us on the telephone, he would show approval for whomever picked up the receiver and said "hello" in Coptic.

Gerges would also teach us new Coptic words and then test us later. There would be praise or monetary rewards for those who did well. And once or twice a fortnight, he would gather all the children and tell us a story in Coptic, whether fictional or about a character from the Bible.

Even when I migrated to Australia with my parents, Gerges would write us letters and aerogrammes in Coptic.

So here are a few hints, gathered from Gerges and other sources, to help keep the language alive: read the Bible and other literature in Coptic; write to yourself and others using Coptic; send text messages in Coptic; and speak to friends and family in Coptic, starting with a few words and then moving to full conversations.

To make the revitalisation or revival work, it is important to renew cultural pride in the language, get family and community support, target children and young people, and use multimedia and videos to teach the language. Coptic should also be a compulsory subject for all pupils, from kindergarten to high school, in Coptic schools.

If Copts take these measures, then Coptic can regain its place as an everyday language.

~~~~~~

Ounas Gerges *is a senior lecturer in the Coptic language at Pope Shenouda III Coptic Theological College, Sydney, Australia.*

17. THE ROLE OF ADVOCACY IN THE CHURCH

Bishop Angaelos

Humanity was created by God in His image and likeness (Genesis 1:27). Not only was all humanity created equal to one another, but it was also endowed with an intrinsic freedom of choice. When humanity fell, our Lord Jesus Christ came to offer us salvation and reconciliation through His Crucifixion and Resurrection from the dead. His sacrifice was a gift to humanity, not imposed, but rather presented to those who choose to accept Him as God Incarnate, believing in Christ as their King and Saviour.

Focusing on the ministry of our Lord Jesus Christ during His time on Earth, we see that He was an advocate for those who were oppressed, marginalised, and outcast by society. Yet we also witness that He made Himself the chief advocate for mankind as a whole (1 John 2:1; Romans 8:34).

At the start of His ministry, our Lord Jesus Christ defined His role and mission on Earth saying, "The Spirit of the Lord is upon Me, because He has anointed Me to preach the gospel to the poor; He has sent Me to heal the broken hearted, to proclaim liberty to the captives and recovery of sight to the blind, to set at liberty those who are oppressed" (Luke 24:8).

When we look at the people with whom our Lord interacted and sought to help, we find characters such as the Samaritan woman (John 4), Matthew the tax collector (Matthew 9:9–11), Mary Magdalene (Luke 8:2; Matthew 27:56), the paralytic (Matthew 9:1–8), and many more.

Although society rejected all these people as outcasts, our Lord Jesus Christ chose to defend and help them.

The fabric of our society is fashioned from different people in various circumstances, but underneath the veneer—at the core of every person and intrinsic to our nature—is that image and likeness of God mentioned above. Out of His deep love and concern for His children, God cannot stand to see any person suffering oppression or marginalisation (2 Corinthians 7:6; Deuteronomy 31:6; Joshua 1:5; Psalm 94:14; Psalm 146:7). Through His love, He calls us to be ambassadors (2 Corinthians 5:20), to follow in His footsteps (Matthew 16:24; John 12:26; 1 Peter 2:21), and to help the poor, captive, and broken hearted. Based on this calling, it is the responsibility of Christians and the Church to imitate the life of its Shepherd. It is our duty to advocate on behalf of all humanity, especially those who are unable to help themselves.

Politics versus advocacy

Two basic misconceptions arise when considering the issue of politics and the Church. The first relates to separating the Church's pastoral role from her advocacy in matters of equality, human rights, and civil liberties, while the other confuses advocacy with political activity and activism.

The definition of *advocacy*, according to the *Oxford English Dictionary*, is "public support for or recommendation of a particular cause or policy", whereas the definition of *political activity* is "the art or science of government or governing, especially the governing of a political entity, such as a nation, and the administration and control of its internal and external affairs".

When we explore the Church's role, we need to distinguish between *politics* and *advocacy*. The Church has a responsibility to speak for the rights and freedoms of her children and the world at large, when those rights are threatened or removed. Meanwhile, the Church should neither side with a particular political party or agenda nor interfere with the running of a nation or state institutions. Religion and faith should be the moral compass of politics and, as a Church, we should be able to speak out for justice, equality, and human rights—ideals forming the core of our faith.

The Church's principle function is to care for her flock, and one way it achieves this is through prayer, whether it is for its own members, the wider community, or the world at large. Even at times of greatest difficulty, prayer is essential, as illustrated in scripture (Philippians 4:6): "Be anxious for nothing, but in everything by prayer and supplication, with thanksgiving, let your requests be made known to God." Accordingly, since the 2011 uprising in Egypt, there have been numerous local, regional, and international calls to prayer.

Along with prayer, Church advocacy is displayed in various ways. These include performing benevolent acts for the needy, speaking on behalf of the underprivileged or alienated or marginalised, and voicing her view on social matters, policies, and laws that might have a detrimental effect. If we turn to recent developments in Egypt, it becomes evident that the Church has spoken out on matters of persecution and injustice on behalf of those whose opinions and voices are often disregarded or silenced.

Our Lord alerts us in John 16:33 that, as Christians, we will face tribulation and persecution in the world: "These things I have spoken to you, that in Me you may have peace. In the world you will have tribulation; but be of good cheer, I have overcome the world." Yet He instructs us in Luke 14:27 to joyfully carry our cross in order to be His disciples. At the same time, we are asked in Galatians 6:2 to imitate Him in helping to alleviate the suffering of others and to "bear one another's burdens, and so fulfil the law of Christ."

The matter of advocacy is also addressed in a recent joint study released by the World Council of Churches, the World Evangelical Alliance, and the Pontifical Council for Interreligious Dialogue of the Roman Catholic Church. The study, which is titled "Christian Witness in a Multi-Religious World", recommends that in the realm of religious freedom and belief, Christians are called to serve others justly and with love, acknowledging the presence of Christ in all humanity (Matthew 25:45). The study also suggests that acts of justice, advocacy, and service, such as providing education and healthcare, should form a part of a common witness to the Gospel of Christ. Furthermore, various recommendations are made, including directing Christians to "cooperate with other religious communities engaging in interreligious advocacy towards justice and the common good and, where possible, standing together in solidarity with people who are in situations of conflict." Christians are also asked to "call on their governments to ensure that freedom of religion is properly and comprehensively respected, recognizing that in many countries religious institutions and persons are inhibited form exercising their mission."[68]

Consequently, Church advocacy plays an integral role in spreading the Gospel of Christ. It is also worth noting that the Coptic Orthodox Church has endured centuries of persecution, whereby it responded with prayer, advocacy, and pastoral care. Our Lord Jesus Christ never retaliated violently to injustice or oppression; likewise, His Church, in Egypt and elsewhere, rejects and condemns the use of violence.

The Maspero Massacre

One of the most poignant moments in recent memory occurred on 9 October 2011, when 26 people lost their lives while peacefully and legally demonstrating on the streets of Cairo. The events that happened that evening have come to be known as the *Maspero Massacre*. Because of the brutal killing of her children by security forces and fanatic militants, the Church exercised her role in advocating for those whose right to life was taken from them on that night. In a statement released in the United Kingdom shortly after the tragic event, the Coptic Orthodox Church highlighted the lack of state protection for Egypt's Christians as they faced escalating violence.[69] This statement also called for an investigation into the excessive use of force by the army, the unresolved attacks on Christians and churches, and the irresponsible and inflammatory coverage by state media. To quote from the statement,

> This is indeed a turning point in Egypt's contemporary history. A time at which there can be positive reform and the building of a new Egypt that is cohesive and that instils a sense of citizenship, ownership and responsibility into every Egyptian, ceasing to focus on the person's religion, but more on his or her contribution and accountability to a single nation state. Alternatively, this can be a point at which we merely continue denying the reality of the presence of conflict, leaving unlawful acts unresolved and unprosecuted, presenting one part of the

---

[68] See "Christian Witness in a Multi-Religious World: Recommendations for Conduct", The Pontifical Council for Interreligious Dialogue of the Roman Catholic Church, the World Council of Churches, and the World Evangelical Alliance, 28 June 2011.

[69] The statement can be viewed at <http://bishopangaelos.org/node/449>. This webpage was accessed on 30 April 2013.

community as a justifiable target, and continuing to drive a wedge between members of a single society, and this will lead to the demise of all.

The Church has a responsibility to voice opinions on matters such as these—and, in so doing, the Church can help to maintain the presence of God in society, infusing His values of love, forgiveness, and faithfulness into the greater community. This benefits everyone, regardless of his or her religion.

Voicing such demands for justice and equality is by no means political activity. Rather, it is part of the Church's calling to defend every citizen's basic rights—rights that were granted by God Himself.

National identity

While we as Christians consider the heavenly Jerusalem as our ultimate destination—the place of our everlasting life with God (Philippians 3:20)—we also live in the world and are members of earthly groupings that form a part of our identity.

Along with the right to defend basic human rights, the Church celebrates a person's identity as a free citizen with equal rights in his or her country of residence. On 24 June 2012, Egyptian State officials announced that Mohamed Morsi was the new president of Egypt, having taken office after an arduous popular uprising that saw the deaths of many for the sake of freedom. On the same day, the Coptic Orthodox Church Centre's Media and Public Relations Office in the United Kingdom issued a press release with my statement outlining the following:

> We pray that God grant him [President Mohamed Morsi] wisdom to govern Egypt and her people, and hope this heralds a smooth transition to continuing democracy, leading to positive reform and the building of a new ethos that is cohesive, instilling a sense of citizenship, ownership and responsibility into every Egyptian. This is the time for Egypt to become a nation that does not focus on a person's religious or political stance, but more on his or her contribution and accountability to a single nation state and equality before the law.
>
> We call for an Egypt for all, one that takes into consideration the value and rights of every citizen, and pray for the new president as he takes on this responsibility. We hope that throughout his service, it is the good of the people of Egypt that will always be core to the decisions he makes at this formative stage and throughout his period in office.[70]

While expectations of the president are made clear in the statement in accordance with the core Christian principles of freedom and basic human rights, it is not against our faith to expect equal and fair treatment to be given to all citizens of a country. It is also important to note, along with the demands made, that a firm understanding of God's protection and sovereignty is expressed and that the fate of His children is understood to be in His hands. Accordingly, the statement asserted that we are confident Egypt is a land blessed by God, Who has promised that He will keep her and her people close to His heart. And, for this reason, we are assured that in the years ahead, He will continue to safeguard and protect her people and lead them to a greater good.

Overall, as Christians and citizens of the country in which we live, we have a responsibility to exercise our God-given right as free individuals to play a constructive part in our country's future, letting our light so shine that others may give glory to God (Matthew 5:16) and being the "salt of the Earth" (Matthew 5:13) that we may give the required flavour for a godly life. We are summoned to be those who live and call for love, forgiveness, reconciliation, and the protection of the vulnerable.

A city set on a hill
In every aspect of our lives, in good times and bad, we are taught in scripture and we see in the life and practice of the Coptic Orthodox Church over the past 2000 years that prayer is essential. We pray to give thanks to God for His creation and all that He has done and continues to do for it, and we also call upon Him during times of trial and tribulation, asking that He either resolve the issue or grant us grace, power, and resilience to persevere. This sometimes needs to happen in conjunction with practical action.

Whether speaking on matters of justice, social issues, human rights violations, or basic freedoms and rights of individuals, the Church has a key role to play in making known the values and principles laid down by our Lord Jesus Christ. We are asked to be a "city set on a hill" so that we may be "the light of the world" (Matthew 5:14). In making

---

[70] The statement can be viewed at <http://copticcentre.blogspot.com.au/2012_06_01_archive.html>. This webpage was accessed on 30 April 2013.

visible its views, we, as the Body of Christ, spread the light and love of God across the world, providing a source of hope for all.

~~~~~~

His Grace Bishop Angaelos is the General Bishop of the Coptic Orthodox Church in the United Kingdom. Born in Cairo, Egypt, and later emigrating to Australia, His Grace obtained his Bachelor of Arts, majoring in political science, philosophy, and sociology. He completed his postgraduate studies in law, before being delegated to the United Kingdom by the late Pope Shenouda III.

Bishop Angaelos is involved in ecumenical and public relations initiatives and travels around the world lecturing to Coptic youth. His Grace holds seats on several bodies dedicated to the ecumenical movement and has appeared on many media outlets expressing his views on post-revolutionary Egypt.

18. NOT OF THIS WORLD

Father Antonios Kaldas

How should the Christian respond to persecution? And how has the Coptic Orthodox Church responded throughout history?

The answer to the first question appears fraught with contradictions. On the one hand, we have the unique Gospel message that enjoins us to love our enemies and to do good to those who persecute us—to turn the other cheek. Yet, on the other hand, the Bible commands us to defend the poor, the downtrodden, and the helpless against those who would take advantage of them. Should Christians fight back against persecution or just accept it meekly? I believe a composite approach exists that unites the two apparently contradictory dictums.

Christianity is not about being weak; it is about being strong. But Christ's strength was not the kind of strength that made Him fight back and defeat His enemies by force. His strength is summarised in a quote attributed to St John Chrysostom, an Early Church Father who lived during the fourth and fifth centuries: "There is a very good way to be rid of your enemy: that is to turn him into a friend."

The central message of the Christian Gospel is *love*. The Christian does not fight his enemy into submission but loves his enemy into transformation. This is what Christ did by submitting to the violent evil of His enemies: He won converts even from among those who crucified Him. This is what the martyrs did by submitting courageously and joyously to torture and death: they won converts even from among the soldiers and pagan onlookers, who saw in their noble martyrdom the essence of truth and the power of love that conquers death.

Love is the most powerful force in all the cosmos. The one who practises love does not practise weakness but strength. The meekness of love is not because the Christian is unable to do otherwise—Christ could have called down 12 legions of angels to save Him from the cross. Rather, the Christian chooses the meek path, motivated by divine unselfish love for others. In this spirit did Christ hold the soldier who slapped Him for no reason to account. Out of love, the Christian withstands her enemies without violence, without insult, without ill will. Yet she withstands all the same, standing firm for truth and justice, if her enemies are working for evil and injustice. Mahatma Gandhi, inspired partly by Christ, triumphed against oppression using nonviolent resistance. Should not such actions inspire true followers of Christ to do the same today?

And if love is combined with truth and justice, it becomes even more powerful. When we stand for the truth that all human beings are created free and are equally valued and loved by God, we are on solid ground. When we strive to achieve genuine freedom from religious persecution and discrimination, we can feel confident that we are toiling for something worthwhile. These struggles give our lives meaning.

Some respond, "But we are not of this world. This world and its problems are not our concern, for we are citizens of heaven. We know this world can never be fixed, so we should focus our efforts on preparing for the next." I believe this is the opposite of what Orthodox Christianity teaches us. For it is written, God created the world and proclaimed it to be *good*. Truth, beauty, majesty—all these wonders fill the world and reflect His nature. Human beings also reflect His nature. And even though the world fell into corruption and decay, evil has managed to graze only the surface of the goodness God created. So when we say that we are strangers and sojourners in this world, we are speaking of the foreignness of the evil that is in the world, not of the actual world itself. When God brings about a "new heaven and a new earth" at the end of time, He will not be destroying the whole of His creation. He will be renewing it, purging it of the evil that has infected His perfect creation. In the mean time, the Church exists on the Earth to participate in that process of renewal and restoration—little piece by little piece. We are to restore the nature of human relationships by imbuing them, once again, with the selfless divine love that originally characterised them.

Others respond by saying it is good to suffer persecution. Christ blesses those who suffer by granting them heavenly rewards. Persecution is good for us, they say. Although this is acceptable for the individual who chooses this lofty spiritual path, does a person have the right to choose it for others? You may, on principle, choose to submit to a mugger on the street, empathising with his desperate circumstances, but do you have the right to leave him to mug an old lady? It is wrong to escape our social responsibility for one another by invoking ascetic spirituality; this is a gross misuse of something that was never intended to be used in such a way. It is also a lie to call something good, when it is evil. Persecution is never good. To be sure, God may produce good results from persecution, contrary to the evil power that causes it, but that still does not make the evil itself good. We rejoice in the cancer patient who repents, but we would consider it immoral to expose people to radiation so that they get cancer and repent. Disease is evil, a result of the fallenness of this world. And we must always fight disease. Oppression and persecution fall under the same category as disease.

Still, others respond that we should only pray. It is not for us to go out and protest and complain and make noise. If God wants to fix this injustice, He does not need us. He is capable of fixing it on His own. And that is, to some extent, true: God does not *need* us to do His will on earth. But He chooses to leave human beings free in their will—free in their choices to do good or evil, to practise love or hate. He does not intervene by giving every suicide bomber a heart attack just before strapping on the dynamite. In this fallen world, where all humans have free will, God works through the free will of His own Body: the Body of Christ. Two thousand years ago, that Body was a single man walking the Earth in Palestine. Today, that same Body is the Church, and we are all its members. It is through our lips that He speaks out for truth and justice. It is through our hands that He carries out works of compassion. It is through our intervention that He protects the unprotected and feeds the hungry. He made this clear when He told us that in the final judgment, we shall be judged according to how we treated those less fortunate than us. For in loving them, we are loving Him, and this love needs to be practical. What good is it, the Apostle James tells us, if we see someone hungry and wish him well but do nothing to feed him? Or what good is it, if we stumble across someone who is oppressed and wish him well yet do nothing to improve his situation?

I believe that the Copts in modern times are not doing too much against injustice but too little. In true Christianity, one does not distinguish between Jew and Gentile, male and female, free and captive. Christian love is love for all humans, indeed, for all creation. Yet when Copts have decided to take a stand against persecution, injustice, and discrimination, it has usually been to protect their own flesh and blood, the Coptic Christians of Egypt. As I have said above, this is good and right. But if we are truly acting out of love for justice and compassion, then why are we Copts strident about the persecution of other Copts yet silent about the many other arenas of persecution that are unfolding right now all over the world? If we are acting out Christian love, should we not be just as outraged about, say, the oppression of the Muslim Rohingya minority in Burma or the persecution of Buddhists in Tibet?

In response, one might say who else would speak out for Egypt's Copts if not their fellow Copts? To which I wholeheartedly agree. Of all the people in the world, it is we Copts in the diaspora who must stand up for our persecuted brothers and sisters in Egypt. This charge falls upon us. But I would argue that our voices might carry more weight, with the world community and the Muslim community in Egypt, if we also took a stand against persecution in all its forms, including the persecution of Muslims. Without such an inclusive stand, we sound like a self-interested group just trying to look after its own. With an inclusive stand, we become an unbiased group that cares about the principle of the matter rather than bland self-interest. Where are the Copts working with and for Amnesty International? Where are the Copts contacting their local Muslim societies to express their concern and sadness over the sad state of persecuted Muslims in the world and standing in solidarity with them as an unjustly persecuted people?

It is only by rising above coarse self-interest to the nobility of principles like the value of human freedom and compassion for all that we can find the strength to overcome that selfish streak that runs through all persecutions. And how are we to expect that transformation in others, if we do not model it ourselves?

Christian love is transformational, not only of individual people but of societies as a whole. It has the power to change hearts and minds and lives and cultures. It is rooted in truths that every human being on this Earth knows deep in their hearts regardless of their creed. And it has the power to transform the persecutor and sustain the persecuted.

In Christ, the Copts find the joy, peace, and confidence that render all temporal disasters powerless to destroy the spirit. In this serenity of invincible confidence and divine love, the Copts stand for truth, justice, and equality in post-revolutionary Egypt as they have for centuries past.

Rarely have Copts embraced violent means to stand up for their rights—and, whenever they have, it has always ended badly. This is not our way. Fanatical Islamists who are convinced that Egypt's Coptic monasteries are brimming with stockpiled automatic weapons and warfare-trained monks are living in a fantasyland constructed from their own fears and violent natures. If they understood the true nature of Christianity, they would realise just how ludicrous such ideas are.

Many observers have said that the survival—and flourishing—of the Coptic faith in Muslim Egypt for 14 centuries is nothing short of a miracle. This claim might contain some truth, given the disintegration of so many other Christian communities in the Islamic Middle East. Yet it is a miracle that continues to unfold even today—the miracle of the power of love over that of brute force.

~~~~~~

Father Antonios Kaldas emigrated to Australia at the age of four years. He serves as a parish priest at Archangel Michael and St Bishoy Coptic Orthodox Church in Mount Druitt, Sydney, and is the Director of St Mark's Coptic Orthodox College in Wattle Grove. He blogs at <http://www.frantonios.org.au>.

19. The Valuable Role of Monasteries in Preserving Coptic Traditions

Bishop Anba Daniel

The Copts, being descendants of the Ancient Egyptians, continued to contribute to the world following the demise of the Ancient Egyptian dynasty. Amongst their many achievements is the establishment of monasticism, which is perhaps one of the most important contributions to Christianity.

Saint Anthony is the father of monasticism. Born in Upper Egypt to wealthy parents around 251 AD, he was orphaned at the age of 18 and was bequeathed with a generous estate. Saint Anthony was inspired by a biblical verse from Luke 18:22:

> When Jesus heard this, he said to him, "You still lack one thing. Sell everything you have and give to the poor, and you will have treasure in heaven. Then come, follow me."

Indeed, Saint Anthony the Great applied the above verse in his life and sold all his possessions and gave them to the poor. He then departed to the desert to live a solitary life in prayer and worship. Many sought to locate him to learn from him and follow his great example. Eventually, rules were established and the world's first Christian monastery was founded near the Red Sea Desert Mountains. This monastery has been revived in recent decades and is one of the most revered Christian sites in all of Egypt, despite its remote location.

The establishment of Coptic monasticism soon saw monasteries flourish not only in Egypt but all over the world. The website of Saint Anthony's Monastery in the United States notes the following important facts, which show the impact that Saint Anthony had on establishing the monastic movement:

Coptic monasticism became known all over the world mainly because of the biography that St. Athanasius wrote about St. Antony. As a result, pious men from many parts of the world flocked to these cenobite monasteries to sit at the feet of those great spiritual giants and learn from them the art of monasticism. Among those were Greeks, Romans, Cappadocians, Libyans, Nubians, Ethiopians and many others. Each nationality was designated a special quarter in each monastery with a fellow citizen as an abbot guide. There were no barriers based on race, culture, color or language. The vastness of the Egyptian desert became but one school of Coptic spirituality and mysticism for the entire world. Some of the greatest personalities of that era were attracted to the Egyptian deserts to see these terrestrial saints and to follow in their footsteps. Among these were St. John Chrysostom, bishop of Constantinople, Sts. Jerome and Rufinus the Italians, the Cappadocian father St. Basil the Great who introduced monasticism into Byzantia, St. John Cassian who carried Coptic Monasticism in France, and many others.

Someone said that monasticism for the Church is like the foundation for the building. The deeper and stronger the foundation is, the more the building can rise high and solid. Ecclesiastical history attests to this reality when it tells us that at times of monastic strength in Egypt, the Church was strong. Through their continual prayers, devotions and mediations, the monks make of their monasteries the powerhouse of the Church. It is a fact that the Coptic Church has suffered a great deal throughout its long history at the hands of Greeks, Romans, Muslims and western missionaries, but through God's grace, the strength of Coptic monasticism has kept the Church still standing as a monument to original Apostolic Orthodox Christianity.[71]

It is known that the Coptic monks had a physical presence in parts of Europe as well. The book *Two thousand years of Coptic Christianity* by Otto FA Meinardus covers in detail the influence of Coptic monasticism in Ireland and Europe. Seven Coptic monks were buried at Disert Ulidh in Ulster and their names are remembered in the litany attributed to Saint Oengus. The book mentions that Saint Anthony,

---

[71] See
<http://www.stantonymonastery.org/index.php?option=com_content&view=article&id=52&Itemid=30>. This webpage was accessed on 25 May 2013.

Celtic monks, and Irish monks are often portrayed with little bells in Celtic art.

As the great River Nile ushers its life-giving waters throughout the Nile Valley so do Coptic monasteries feed the spiritual needs of Copts and Christians throughout the world. Coptic monasteries played an extremely important role in protecting the Coptic culture, including language, art, and theology. Coptic bishops and the Coptic pope are chosen from among the monks, all of whom would have served many years living in solitude in a desert monastery.

In an article titled "A visit to the Depth of the Desert", printed in the *Khaleeg* newspaper (21 November 1988) in the United Arab Emirates, the journalist Ahmed El-Gamal said, "In Anba Bishoy Monastery, I met the fathers—the monks—and I cannot explain the spirituality of the place, nor the hospitality, nor the overflowing Encyclopaedia of education, but it is enough for me to concentrate on the fact that it's a big loss for each Arab to neglect the role of the Christian Monastic Movement in our history without disturbing what is known about the position of the Islamic religion that there is no monasticism in Islam." He also said that each monk is to work to provide for the needs of the monastery, and whatever is in excess is to be given to the needy. In addition to the craft work that each monk must perform, there is other work in the fields of science, for example, improving the art of cultivating the desert, discovering plants suitable for such an environment, and planting natural herbs.

Today, Coptic monasteries are witnessing a revival throughout the world driven mainly by the immigration of Copts. For Coptic migrants, a Coptic monastery completes the spiritual Christian experience, because the newly established monasteries outside of Egypt cater for youth retreats, solitude, and meditation (since most Coptic monasteries are located outside urban areas).

Our monastery in Sydney is named after Saint Shenouda the Archimandrite and is located in the Putty region of New South Wales. The monastery receives guests from around Australia and all over the world. Coptic monasteries have always been a source of blessing and benefit to all whom visit.

~~~~~~

His Grace Bishop Anba Daniel *is Bishop and Abbot of Saint Shenouda's Monastery in Sydney. Prior to becoming Bishop, His Grace served the Coptic Orthodox Church in New Zealand, the Fiji Islands, and all the states of Australia.*

20. THE TRANSFORMATION OF A NATION

Bishop Thomas

Throughout the course of history, Egypt has contributed to almost every civilisation in the world through its applications and implementations of chemistry, architecture, mathematics, astronomy, writing, and papyrus paper—just to name a few examples.

Although the land of Egypt can be considered large by area, much of it is desert and people are forced to live on only six per cent of the whole area of land available. It is these boundaries of geography and climate that push people into small communities and villages to survive and flourish. Consequently, the Nile has created its own importance and relevance to the people living off it. Egyptians have lived and continue to live with this paradox: the life of the Nile surrounded by the bareness of the desert.

Each civilisation in Egypt's history has endured this paradox of superiority and inferiority—past greatness and present depravity. This grand history has given Egyptians two important guiding principles: inclusiveness and a strong sense of identity.

Ancient Egyptians had their own special ideology in dealing with religious conflict, tolerance, and coexistence. Ancient Egyptians would embrace a particular God while honouring a number of other deities at the same time. Right from the beginning they considered themselves religious people, no matter which god they worshiped. Religion in Egypt had always been and continues to be the cornerstone of the Egyptian identity. In pharaonic times, many great achievements were developed in and around the temple, and it was considered a *house of life* where people received their education, learned essential skills, developed a philosophy of life, and built a sense of community.

Nevertheless, Egypt was strongly influenced by foreign invaders and outside powers, who found Egypt to be an attractive location for various empires. This resulted in frequent wars, conquests, and invasions over the centuries, which have left their mark culturally, socially, religiously, and politically on the Egyptian identity. New concepts and perspectives brought in with these foreigners, which were embraced and adopted, added new dimensions to the Egyptian worldview.

After the conquests of Alexander the Great, Egypt came under the influence of the Greco-Roman civilisation. It was only then that Egyptians began to experience the process of becoming part of a larger political body. Egypt was exposed to the new religion, culture, and traditions of the Greco-Roman people, and struggled to maintain the uniqueness of its own civilisation. The Egyptian people's adaptability and acceptance of the new culture caused a merger between the Egyptian and Hellenic civilisations. This led to the extraordinary cosmopolitan environment, which we now know as the city of Alexandria with its libraries, schools, great thinkers, and philosophers.

When Saint Mark came to Alexandria in 52 AD and introduced Christian philosophy, Christianity became an important partner in the development of Alexandria's openness to various philosophies. The city became a home for Christian, Jewish, and Greco-Roman culture. Even though the presence of differing religious ideas sometimes resulted in conflict, the philosophies enriched one another and helped lay the foundation for a concept of coexistence and tolerance in a harmonious manner.

In the seventh century, however, Egypt entered a new era with the Arab conquests. A new culture arrived with a different language, way of life, religion, and political identity. The concept of coexistence that Egyptians had learnt before now helped them cope with these new changes brought on by the Arab conquests. As they adjusted to becoming part of another political and cultural body, they also had to struggle to keep their own Egyptian identity. A conflict arose between the need for coexistence and the preservation of Egyptian identity, in the face of Arabism. This process of Arabisation began to change Egypt's language, customs, and culture. Furthermore, a process of Islamisation began taking place, completely changing the ideology and practices of Egyptians and Christians alike. This process is still ongoing in many ways, and it is continuing to reshape the Egyptian identity, culture, and political ideology.

All aspects of society that had to endure these stages of change were able to keep a small sense of pride and belonging in their own beliefs. But we can see the unique characteristics of each group shift towards a more Arab influence as the pressure to conform increases for the Egyptian people. There were three distinct groups of people who cemented this process of change.

The first group was the initial wave of Arab soldiers who invaded Egypt. These soldiers began to rapidly infiltrate Egypt, as they realised that Egypt had an untapped reservoir of wealth and prosperity, which they exploited when they decided to stay in Egypt and marry the Egyptian women. These soldiers then brought in their Arabian cultures, religion, and political philosophies, which greatly impacted on the Egyptian mentality and way of life. Over time this group started influencing a wider range of Egyptian society as their numbers began to grow.

The second group of people who reformed Egypt's landscape were the Egyptians who converted to Islam through force, pressure, blackmail, or coercion.

The third group chose to reject the Islamisation of Egypt and held fast to their beliefs, along with their true Ancient Egyptian heritage. They were forced to pay for keeping their religion and identity. These people are known as the Copts. This term was derived from Egypt's pharaonic name *Ke-Pe-Tah*, and was translated by the Greeks into *Egyptos*, which the Arabs then pronounced as *Gept*. Arabs in Egypt used this term, *Gept*, to refer to the original Egyptians as a whole, and then used it to refer to Egyptians who remained Christian. The Copts carried with them many legacies that were distinct from Arab traditions, such as the old Egyptian language, calendar, culture, and art. This heritage is not only an important part of Egypt's identity, but it also represents a valuable era of ancient human civilisation. Therefore, Copts feel the world should take responsibility to conserve this heritage, because it carries a unique message and meaning for all humanity.

The Copts had to endure three distinctive yet complex processes during the Arabisation of Egypt. First, they had to try to find a delicate balance between their Egyptian heritage and identity, while trying to integrate in a rapidly growing Arabic culture. For instance, they had to try to maintain their Coptic language, while learning to use the country's new official language of Arabic. Second, they had to balance their loyalty to their Egyptian heritage and culture, while trying to accept the realities of being part of the Arab world. Third, they had to carefully balance their right to express their Christian identity, while being immersed in an Islamic environment. This pressure to conform to the Islamic–Arabian environment, history, and culture is one which has been passed down from generation to generation and remains a strong part of the Coptic struggle today. Although collectively these struggles continue to be a source of conflict for the Copts today, the political climate and demand for democracy and state autonomy has opened the door for Copts to hope for a more accepting and tolerant Egypt.

On 25 January 2011, the people of Egypt began to protest against the rule of former President Hosni Mubarak. Their demands included basic human rights, freedom, democracy, and social justice. A majority of people in Egypt were delighted by this new turn of events, and the famous Tahrir Square in central Cairo was filled with many people expressing the hope for transformation. People from different backgrounds—men and women, Christians and Muslims, rich and poor—united with one another to change society. The chance to create a new and better Egypt kept them in Tahrir Square for 18 days as they demonstrated for an idealistic yet essential dream of democracy.

Over a year has passed since Mubarak resigned his post, yet an old but familiar struggle has re-emerged in Egypt—a struggle in which a few wish to establish a religious state based on Islam. It can already be seen that Egypt is undergoing many transformations, and the society appears to be drifting towards two larger groups with two very different visions. One group is working for the establishment of an Islamic state, and the other is working for an open, civil state. A few observers say that the protesters who took to the streets in January 2011 have not achieved their objectives or even reaped the rewards of their struggles. They also say that these youth have opened the door to other more extremist forces to take power. However, despite the empowerment of Islamist movements in parliamentary and presidential elections, the spirit of those Egyptians working for an open, civil society is still strong. The fire of freedom and equality is in the hearts of many Egyptians, and it will not be put out easily.

The Coptic community has aligned itself with those who are striving for a civil and open society—those who hope for a real transformation of the nation in three crucial aspects of society.

The first aspect involves the transformation or evolution of a hierarchal Egyptian society into a more democratic one. The country must be transformed from the rule of one authoritative dictatorship into the rule of a democratic government. Egyptian society needs to move towards a system based on a constitutional government that empowers all. To do this, the society should be transformed from its grass roots so that it can practise democracy in its true form. This will take place at home in the family and even at work, and will involve allowing everyone the right to express themselves freely without intimidation or suppressing the expression of others. This will not happen overnight, and it will also have to be linked to the reformation of the educational system. When society learns to live by the rules of democracy, democracy in politics will inevitably follow. Democracy is not just the rule of the majority, and its application extends to more than just a political system. It is a philosophical change that all levels of society must embrace. It also means accepting the responsibility to guarantee that every individual in society has the freedom and ability to express themselves and their ideology genuinely and with equal opportunity. If democracy starts by working inside people's hearts, then it will carry over and flow into the people's government.

The second aspect is the transformation of a male-dominated society into a society based on gender equality and advancement. Because Egyptian society is currently dominated by patriarchal rule, it is the responsibility of those same men in power to provide the opportunity for women to take their place as equal members in society. Egypt also needs to create a number of programs that empower and educate women, while also informing men about the benefits of giving women equal opportunities. Just as before, it is vital that a reformation and adjustment of the schooling system and educational curriculum is implemented as soon as possible in order for this change to take place.

The third aspect that needs to change is the transformation of a religiously intolerant society into a more open and accepting one. Today, everything in Egypt is subject to religion. Politicised religion is creating a deep segregation in society, even for people holding the same faith. The distance between the open minded, the moderates, and the radicals is rapidly widening. This anticipated transformation towards a society of openness and tolerance will provide an ideal atmosphere that respects the spirituality of the individual without the backlash of vindication. These conditions will encourage cultural expression along with a harmonious and peaceful atmosphere.

The process of transformation in Egypt will need to continue for some time. The Coptic community remains an active partner in this process as it shares the responsibility of spreading peace and creating harmony in the Egyptian society. It is the Coptic community's responsibility to preserve the roots of Egyptian culture and heritage, while remaining faithful to the philosophy of openness and peaceful coexistence.

~~~~~~

His Grace Bishop Thomas *is the Coptic Orthodox Bishop of El-Quosia and Mair in Egypt, and the founder and leader of the Anafora Retreat and Training Centre. His Grace has received three prizes for his work on human rights and freedom of speech: the 1999 Freedom House Prize from the United States, the 2006 Stefanus Prize from Norway, and the 2012 Bjornstjerne Bjornson Prize from Norway.*

21. COPTS AND IMMIGRATION

The Very Rev. Father Tadros El-Bakhoumi

Copts are the descendants of the pharaohs and Ancient Egyptians, the original inhabitants who resided in Egypt thousands of years before the birth of our Lord God and Saviour Jesus Christ.

The word "Coptic", from its linguistic roots, means *Egyptian*. To understand how it came about, one must take into account that it is common place to formally recognise a country by the name of its capital city. For instance, when you are going to England, you usually say, "I am booking my ticket to London." In the same manner, approximately 400 years before the birth of Christ, the capital of Egypt at that time was known as *Hiktou-Petah*, which means *the house of the Egyptian God, Petah*. When the Greeks occupied Egypt about 300 years before Christ, they could not pronounce the name *Hiktou-Petah* in their language, so they changed it to *Egyptah*, from which came the word "Egyptian". This consequently gave rise to the name of the country: Egypt.

The name "Egyptian" comes from the Coptic language. It is the modern derivative, *Kimee*, of the ancient Heliographic language of the Pharaohs, and represents the main inhabitants of the land. When the Muslims of Arabia invaded Egypt, they were unable to use the word "Egyptian" in their Arabic language, so they used the term "*Gypt*". Later on, when the Europeans invaded Egypt, they took the word "*Gypt*" that was used by the Muslim Arabians to be Coptic, and since then it transformed into the word "Copt" to express the original inhabitants of the land of Egypt. So the use of the word "Copt" in this chapter will be taken to mean the person who is originally of Egyptian blood, regardless of his or her religion.

From their forefathers, the pharaohs, the Copts inherited a great civilisation. It is well known that the Ancient Egyptians were highly advanced in science, astronomy, civil engineering, medicine, geometry, chemistry, ship making, and embalming. Till now, even our modern science with all its latest technological advancements has not been able to unravel some of the secrets of the Ancient Egyptians.

Saint Mark the Apostle, and the author of the second Gospel in the Bible, arrived in Alexandria in 42 AD. Thus began the building of the great monasteries and churches, which still stand today and attract tourists from around the world.

By nature, the Copts are a religious people who hold firmly to their faith—before and after Christianity came to exist. As for the original Coptic Christians, the history books bear witness to their steadfastness in their religion, even when many shed their blood for the sake of Christ.

The Copts escaped bloodshed by dwelling in monasteries. The monastic life in Egypt started in the first century, but only existed in little groups dotted throughout the deserts of Egypt. From the time of Emperor Constantine, and after the move of Saint Anthony the Great (the father of monks in the eastern deserts) and "Saint Bakhomios the great father of community" in the southern deserts, the monastic life has flourished dramatically with thousands of monks leaving everything for the love of Christ and giving their lives to Him. It increased so dramatically to the extent that Saint Jerome, in his visit to Egypt, made a statement that the person who travels from Alexandria (far north of Egypt) to Aswan (far south of Egypt) through the deserts will be continuously hearing the praises of the monks along the whole way.

In the seventh century, the Arabian Muslims of the Middle East invaded Egypt by the sword and the Coptic Christians kept their way of peace and did not fight back.

Since the Arabian Islamic invasion, the Egyptian Copts, who were all Christians since 42 AD, began to face a barrage of persecution, which occurred more frequently and became more violent year by year. The blood of the innocent Christians, which was shed over the years since the Islamic invasion in the seventh century, is boundless and still continues today. They were trying by all means to force the Coptic

Christians to embrace Islam, but many never accepted it.

The Islamic persecution and pressure on the Coptic Christians in Egypt continued to increase until the twenty-first century. The persecution was in every aspect of life; it was against any person with a Christian name and took place in schools, universities, public jobs, police forces, armies, trades, and many other walks of life. It was due to this suffering that many Copts began to leave Egypt in order to find a safe place to live and experience the basic rights of a free citizen. The immigration of the Coptic Christians started in the late 1950s. Many departed to the United States, the United Kingdom, Australia, Canada, and Europe. The immigration of the 1950s and 1960s was during the time of President Gamal Abdel Nasser, who managed to slightly minimise this suffering due to his strong relationship with Pope Kyrillos VI, as the Pope managed to save his life by forewarning him of a threat. Since this incident, President Nasser respected Pope Kyrillos VI and the persecution was not as rampant.

After president Nasser came President Anwar El-Sadat. He was a member of the fanatic Islamic Brotherhood of Egypt, and this was the most difficult time for Coptic Christians. The persecution got out of control. Many forms of abuse began to take place, such as burning of churches, attacking and killing Christians in their villages and homes, looting their shops, firing them from their jobs, limiting their participation in managerial and bureaucratic jobs, and restricting their placement in government and judicial appointments. In brief, the persecution was extreme, and there were few laws to protect Christian rights. Accordingly, during the dark period of President Sadat, immigration increased rapidly.

After I came to Australia in 1986, I felt obligated to start a special programme, apart from the normal channels of immigration, to save the lives of innocent Christians and get them out of Egypt. From 1986 to 1991, I met with ministers of immigration, politicians, and parliamentary members to present the case and seek a solution. What resulted was the approval from the Hon. Jerry Hand to start a special visa programme specifically for Egypt's persecuted Christians. This programme worked well and helped many people who were under threat. And the programme continues today. It gives people hope and a new life.

As mentioned earlier, many Coptic Christians are religious. So after settling abroad, Copts began establishing churches, schools, theological colleges, and monasteries.

After the 2011 Egyptian Revolution, many hoped the democratic election of a new president would bring about a fair and civil government that would apply freedom and justice to all Egyptians, regardless of their faith or worldview. However, sadly, the Muslim Brotherhood and other Islamic fanatics like the Salafists overtook this position by means of unfair elections and now Egypt is once again entering another era of Islamic reign. This is causing many riots and much bloodshed in the streets. These demonstrations have been witnessed by many people on the Internet and have damaged the immigration status of Copts. Every time they approach the Australian Embassy requesting a visa for visitation, they are rejected based on the belief that they are trying to flee Egypt.

In conclusion, Egypt, which was once a beautiful and safe country and a major tourist hub, has now changed into a place of fear and intimidation. Tourism is dead. We ask God to have mercy on Egypt and remove the Islamic fundamentalists. We also ask God to stop the persecution of innocent Egyptians, so that they may live in peace and harmony like any other person around the world.

~~~~~~

The Very Reverend Father Tadros El-Bakhoumi, OAM, is the Parish Priest of Saint Mary, Saint Bakhomios, and Saint Shenouda Coptic Orthodox Church in Kirrawee, Sydney. He is also a chaplain with the Department of Corrective Services, serving all prisoners in New South Wales.

Since 1987, Father Tadros has been teaching systematic theology, ritual theology, and dogmatic-traditional theology at the Coptic Orthodox Theological College in Sydney.

22. COPTS THROUGHOUT THE AGES—A SNAPSHOT

Peter Tadros

Egypt is the cradle of civilisation. The legacy of the pharaohs and the wonders of Ancient Egypt continue to fascinate the world, even until today. Millions of tourists travel to Egypt to witness the Great Pyramids and ancient temples, which remain standing as a testimony of a glorious past. Universities across the globe offer courses as well as doctorates, and each year thousands of students eagerly enrol to learn more about the great ancient people of Egypt and its civilisation, which commenced approximately 6000 years ago.

The following excerpt from an article by archaeologist Aidan Dobson sums up Egypt: "As a field for scholarly research, or simply a holiday destination, Egypt remains imprinted on the world's consciousness in a way hardly equalled by any other ancient society, centuries after its culture apparently vanished from the Earth."[72]

It would be negligent of any writer or author of a book on the Coptic people not to mention the connections back to Ancient Egypt. The Copts of Egypt are the direct descendants of the Ancient Egyptians. The Copts are the native people of Egypt, and they are its aborigines.

---

[72] For more information, see
<http://www.bbc.co.uk/history/ancient/egyptians/egypt_end_01.shtml>. This webpage was accessed on 31 May 2013.

The term "Copt" refers to the Egyptian Christians who were evangelised by Saint Mark the Apostle in the first century AD. The word probably originates from the old-Egyptian word "*Hwt-Ka-Ptah*", which means the *House of the God Ptah*. While the Greeks used the word "*Aigyptos*" for Egypt, the Copts used the Coptic term "*Kyptos*".[73]

So why has this culture seemingly vanished? What remains of the mighty Egyptian culture besides the Great Pyramids, the Temple of Karnak, and other ancient monuments?

The Coptic calendar was the first calendar in the world, and it was established by the great astronomer Toot in 4241 BC. The following is an excerpt from "The Coptic New Year EL-Nayrouz Feast of the Martyrs", an article written by the Sydney-based the Very Reverend Father Tadros El-Bakhoumi:

> When one looks at the historical persecutions in Egypt, the number of Christians who were martyred in Egypt is far greater than any other country throughout the whole world. It is also known that the Roman Emperors and kings persecuted Christians, especially those of Egypt and the Middle East. One of those kings was Diocletian whose reign started in the year 284 AD and ended in 305 AD.
>
> During this time the greatest number of Christian Egyptians were killed as Diocletian declared that he would continue killing the Christians of Egypt till their blood fills the streets and reaches the knees of his horse.
>
> As a result of numerous Christians martyred during the reign of Diocletian, the Coptic Orthodox Church in Egypt reset the Coptic calendar and established another name for the Coptic New Year, this being "The year of Martyrs". At that time the entire Egyptian population were Christians.

The Coptic Calender is still in use today by the Coptic Orthodox Church, making it one of the oldest calendars in the world.

The Ancient Egyptians and the Copts were patriots and proud of their heritage and beliefs. In this chapter, we hope to unveil the mysteries of Egypt's history that we do not read or learn much about, and we shall try to fill in the gaps on important issues such as Egypt since the Arab-Islamic invasion that occurred around 640 AD.

In recent times, there have been requests to include the Coptic Era, or the era prior to the Arab-Islamic invasion, in the Egyptian educational curriculum. The Coptic era does not exist, judging from the Egyptian Government's current educational curriculum, as it has been

---

[73] For more information, see <http://www.coptic-cairo.com/culture/culture.html>. This webpage was accessed on 31 May 2013.

purposefully omitted from the record. There is a lot of church history engulfed in the rich Coptic era from the day the Apostle Saint Mark first evangelised Christianity in Egypt till the years following the end of the Diocletian persecutions. So the question must be asked: how much do we know about the status of Copts during the Arab-Islamic era? After all, it was this era that shaped the fortunes of Egypt's Copts.

In 2010, the Reverend Dr Mark Durie wrote a book titled *The Third Choice*. This book discusses the widening impact of sharia revival and the deterioration of human rights in Islamic societies. In his book, Durie says that the Coptic Church holds minimal records on any Coptic analyses of Islam. This is astonishing considering the Arabs invaded and conquered Egypt since 640, and remain there until this day.

The oral tradition is very strong among Copts, although there is a great need to objectively look at the conditions of the Copts following the Greco-Roman era and up until the modern era. Some radical changes occurred during this era following the Arab conquest, and these events have changed Egypt dramatically—and, of course, changed the fortunes of Egypt's indigenous Coptic population.

The Byzantines were in control of Egypt just prior to the Arab conquest, and there was growing discontent among the native Egyptian population against the harsh treatment they were receiving from their rulers. 'Amr ibn al-'As was the Arab military leader who led the Muslim conquest of Egypt in 640.[74] He had prior knowledge of the country, since he was a trader. Jacques Tagher in *Christians in Muslim Egypt* recounts the atmosphere at the time of the Arab conquest:

> 'Amr ibn al-'As, like Alexander, knew that the people wanted new rulers. He also knew that the country was not well-fortified and that he could easily invade it. In this light, he invaded with the 3500–4000 soldiers put at his disposal by the caliph 'Umar.
>
> The Byzantine army consisted of 23,000 men however the key for the Arab invaders was that they were under a unified leadership and attacked in large numbers and the Byzantines did not have a plan for defense based on cooperation between governors. The Copts of Egypt were totally absent from the scene crushed by their Byzantine rulers.

---

[74] See <http://en.wikipedia.org/wiki/%27Amr_ibn_al-%27As>. This webpage was accessed on 31 May 2013.

Tagher notes that, at the time of the Arab conquest, the Coptic Patriarch was in exile and the Copts were rather passive after learning of the advance of the Arab armies. Some historians have suggested that the Copts may have supported the invading Arab armies; however, Tagher notes that the siege of the Babylon fortress lasted for a long time, and there is not a single text that indicates the Copts offered any assistance to the invading Arabs. Today, there is a reminder of the Arab army's siege of the fortress of Babylon (in modern-day *Old Cairo*, or *Coptic Cairo*), where the remains of the gates to the fortress still stand in the Coptic quarter of Old Cairo. There were also several Coptic revolts, which were eventually crushed by the Arabs.

To understand what happened in Egypt after the Arab-Islamic conquest, we will need to understand the meaning of *dhimmi* and how Islamic sharia principles were applied to the native Egyptian population who refused to convert to Islam. A *dhimmi* is a person living in a region overrun by Muslim conquest, and is accorded a protected status and allowed to retain his original faith under certain conditions.[75] The following is an excerpt from Tagher's book; the passage describes the restrictions imposed on *dhimmis*:

> Abu Yussuf told the caliph, "To facilitate the collection of the *jizyah*, it is advisable to affix sealable rings on the necks of those liable to pay it as 'Uthman ibn Hanif did. After the completion of the collection, the rings may be removed upon request. They should not be permitted to emulate Muslims in clothes, in riding horses and donkeys, or in their general appearance. They should wear girdles that resemble thick drapes tied around their waists. They should fix a wooden ball in the shape of a pomegranate (on their saddles) instead of the saddle bow, and double-lace their sandals, and should not emulate Muslims. Their women should not be permitted to ride on saddles. They should also be prevented from building new churches in any town except those wherein they had (church buildings) when peace was made with them and they were made *dhimmis*. Whatever belonged to them at the time, of synagogues and churches, should be left with them and should not be demolished. It is likewise in the case of their fireplaces. They should be permitted to live in the towns of the Muslims and in their streets, to buy and sell anything except wine and pigs, and not to make a display of their crosses in the towns."

Tagher also notes that the Arabs knew little of the art of governing, so the management of occupied territories kept them busy. There was a

---

[75] See <http://www.merriam-webster.com/dictionary/dhimmi>. This webpage was accessed on 31 May 2013.

clear lack of plans, and all political, economic, and social decisions were haphazard. There was a lack of consistency on how sharia law was to be applied on the people of the *dhimma*. Public works were almost completely neglected, and the number-one purpose of the new rulers of Egypt was simply to collect more taxes. The Copts were the major source of such taxes.

The application of the *jizyah* on the Copts meant that they would be entitled to protection. The *jizyah* was a poll tax on *dhimmis*, although even the payment of such a tax did not guarantee protection for the Copts throughout the centuries following the Arab conquest. Both oral tradition and scholarly notes confirm that the *dhimmis* of Egypt were given three choices following the Arab conquest: convert to Islam, or pay *jizya* and adhere to its conditions, or die.

According to Tagher, the most blood thirsty of all Egypt's caliphs was 'al-Hakim bi-Amr Allah, who ruled from 996 to 1020. It is said that up to 30,000 churches and monasteries were destroyed during this period. The following passage from Tagher best describes the atmosphere during the caliph's reign:

> It is said that the number of churches and monasteries destroyed was thirty thousand. The savagery of the mob that carried out the wish of their master caused the situation to deteriorate even more. These people actually eradicated churches from the surface of the earth, and their vengefulness reached the point of digging up the bones of dead Christians to use as fuel for their public baths. Later, orders were issued to donkey drivers and boatmen not to transport *dhimmis*.

The years following 'al-Hakim's devastation, and after the attempted crusades, demonstrate a decline in the role and number of the Copts in Egypt. Tagher summarises their predicament, after 'al-Hakim's era, as follows:

> The story of the crusades helps one to understand more clearly the decline of the Copts after the persecutions of al-Hakim bi-'Amr Allah. This condition continued through the reigns of the Mamluk and Turkish sultans who exhibited no (special) interest in the (Coptic) minority. The sultans considered Copts as an integral part of the nation because they rendered valuable services related to tax collection. Moreover the rulers were capable of fleecing money from the minority without fearing a revolutionary movement. In fact, they shaped the destiny of the Copts according to their own whims and those of the general populace.
>
> Some Coptic secretaries were able to occupy high positions in the state. But people used to express their anger when they saw a Copt with influence, as if it

118

were unacceptable that a small religious minority had any rights (to high positions). But a Copt was able to advance to such a situation because his Muslim counterpart "at that time" did not have necessary qualifications, or (seemingly) did not want to seek the qualifications, to collect taxes. Aside from this particular job the Copt felt that he was unwanted. Thus the Coptic community became a group for training specialists in taxes and financial affairs.

The demise of the Coptic language is perhaps one of the great losses for the Egyptian and Coptic cultures. Here is an excerpt from Tagher on this topic:

Egypt spoke Coptic in the seventh century. By the twelfth century all Egypt spoke Arabic. The Arabs were able to make their subjects leave their old language behind and replace it with another, an achievement that the Greeks and Romans were unable to do before them and the Turks were unable to do after them.

Thankfully, there are still a few-hundred Copts worldwide who use the Coptic language in regular conversation, and there is an effort to revive the language of the pharaohs, as you will discover in other chapters in this book. The language is used in the Coptic Church services (along with Greek), although the bulk of the liturgy is either in Arabic or the language of the nation that the church is located in.

Tagher's research shows that the plight of Egypt's Copts did not change during the six centuries preceding Muhammad Ali. Muhammad Ali Pasha was an Albanian commander in the Ottoman army, who became Wāli and the self-declared Khedive of Egypt and Sudan. His reign stretched from 1805 to 1848.[76]

Tagher credits Muhammad Ali's reign as a period when discrimination against Copts subsided and many church-building decrees were issued, although he notes the Copts still did not achieve full equality status.

Muhammad Ali was part of the Ottoman forces sent to expel the French revolutionary expedition of 1798 to 1801. He led the modernisation of Egyptian agriculture, medicine, and technology.[77]

Did the Copts benefit from the ruling French invaders and coreligionists? Tagher's account of the brief French era indicates almost

[76] See <http://en.wikipedia.org/wiki/Muhammad_Ali_of_Egypt>. This webpage was accessed on 31 May 2013.

[77] See <http://www.digitalegypt.ucl.ac.uk/chronology/islamic.html>. This webpage was accessed on 31 May 2013.

no benefit for the Copts. In fact, Napoleon continued the same policies of previous Islamic rulers of Egypt, because he did not want to be seen as favouring the minority Christians over the majority Muslims. Napoleon went to great lengths to appease the Muslim majority, hoping to win their support, as demonstrated in Tagher's book: "To the *sheikhs*, judges, chiefs, imams and the elite of the country: Tell your nation that the French are also sincere Muslims." Furthermore, Napoleon at times spoke harshly about the Copts and referred to them as "hated thieves in the country, but we should care for them because they alone know the general principles of managing the country".

Prior to analysing the British occupation, we should look at Tagher's account of one of the special fields that Copts found themselves controlling. The following is a passage, from Tagher's book, quoting a text from Duke d'Harcout's *L'Egypte et les Egyptiens*:

> Their unique calculating genius made them use the figures according to methods that they had learned through childhood, making very complex calculations based on 1/24, 1/3, 1/4, 1/2, 1/24 out of 1/24. It is difficult for us to follow their method of calculation because they conduct it with great speed, using certain ambiguous abbreviations which are recorded on paper. Undoubtedly we can reach the accurate solution faster than they do by using the methods of calculation followed in Europe. But because their methods are based on measurements in use in the country and because they do not use the decimal fraction system, their speed in their calculations exceeds ours. Due to these complex methods of calculation known to them alone, the Arabs (Muslims) have become dependent on them.

In 1882, the British fully occupied Egypt. Tagher notes that the above remarks concerning the Copts' speciality in administration of financial affairs ended once the British gained control of the country and introduced their own methods.

Kyriakos Mikhail put together a collection of facts in 1911 concerning the Copts. The collection was titled *Copts and Moslems under British Control*, and it aimed at influencing the public opinion on Coptic grievances. Mikhail stated that these facts should be considered fairly and without prejudice so that the British public recognises the previous wrongs committed against Christians in Egypt. This is an excerpt from Mikhail's collection, which was written by Professor AH Sayce:

> The genuine Egyptians are the Christian Copts. They alone trace an unadulterated descent from the race to whom the civilisation and culture of the ancient world

were so largely due. Thanks to their religion, they have kept their blood pure from admixture with semi-barbarous Arabs and savage Kurds, or other foreign elements whom the licentiousness of Mohammedan family life has introduced into the country. In Upper Egypt, it is true, where the conversion of the fellahin to Mohammedanism is a comparatively recent event, there is still a considerable amount of pure Egyptian blood in the Mohammedan part of the population, but even here large tracts were colonised in the Middle Ages by numerous bodies of Arab and Beduins, and when religion ceased to be a barrier to intermarriage, these latter necessarily mingled with the fellahin converts.

In his preface to the collection, Sayce goes on to write that

The neighbourhood of Cairo was colonised by Arab tribes, and the revolts of the Christian fellahin of the Delta during the first few centuries after the Mohammedan occupation were followed by merciless massacres. If we were to discover the real representatives of "Egypt and the Egyptians" we must go to the remnant which has maintained itself through twelve centuries of persecution, more especially in Upper Egypt.

As Professor Flinders Petrie has remarked, the fact that through all these centuries of persecution the Copts should nevertheless have not only maintained themselves, but have even made themselves indispensable to their Mohammaden masters, is both a testimony to their extraordinary ability and proof that they are indeed the children of their Egyptian fathers. They have kept alive the old traditions of education and culture through centuries of darkness, along with the Christian conception of family morality and all that this implies.

Sayce concludes his preface to Mikhail's collection with the following:

During the last thirty years I have seen a good deal of the Coptic people, more especially of the younger generation and I have found them to compare favourably with other nations. They have inherited the aptitudes and intellectual abilities of their forefathers; their morality and conception of the family is that of a Christian people, in other words, of Western European civilisation; and I see no reason why they should not again take the same high place in the civilised world that was taken by their Pharaonic ancestors. Egypt, as Sir Gaston Maspero once said to me, is the mother of most of the ideas that have since ruled the world, and the children of that mother are still with us, under the name of Copts.

The introduction to Mikhail's collection was written by Dr Butler. He shows that the Copts were also shunned by the British:

This little work presents a clear and dispassionate statement of the Coptic grievances and the Coptic claims. I venture strongly to recommend it to all fair minded persons who desire to know the truth, and particularly to those who have been misled by British official reports or utterances into the belief that the grievances of the Copts are shadowy and unreal.

So far is this from being the case, so substantial and so serious are the injustices which the Copts suffer from under British rule, and which in a large measure have been created by British rule, that I do not hesitate to say that their position as an oppressed minority is a standing discredit and reproach to our boasted methods of government. The plan has been to show indiscriminate favour to the Muslims-with the not unnatural result of turning many of them into enemies of England and the English occupation, to treat the Copts with stern disfavour, and to turn a deaf ear to all remonstrance.

The English author Butcher wrote the first chapter in Mikhail's collection, and she titled it "In the House of Bondage". This is an excerpt from her chapter on British rule in Egypt:

It is true that since 1884, the Copts have been freed from all legal disabilities, but persistent favouritism has always been shown to the Moslems, and this had a bad effect both on them and on the Copts. The Moslems attribute our attitude to fear of them, and of late years a movement has been got up, principally by descendants of those very Turks who were the worst governors and oppressors that Egypt ever knew, in favour of "Nationalism", though the bulk of the nation, Moslem and Christian alike, would repudiate it if they dared, and would suffer greatly if this new intrigue of the Turks succeeded.

This chapter is by no means a comprehensive summary of Coptic history, although it does shed some light on a people who have suffered persecution for close to 2000 years. It is astonishing to read the history in light of today's events in Egypt. Unfortunately, nothing much has changed. Since 1952, attacks against Coptic Christians have continued, including mob violence, destruction of churches, massacres of Coptic protestors, and the ongoing disappearance of Coptic women. At the time of writing this chapter, a new constitution has just been passed in Egypt. It was almost entirely drafted by Islamists, members of the Muslim Brotherhood, and the ultraradical Salafists.

Could we be returning to the era of 'al-Hakim bi-Amr Allah? Or will the Copts finally be afforded full citizenship, along with their Muslim-Arab counterparts?

~~~~~~

Peter Tadros *has participated in fact-finding missions and presented at many seminars. He features regularly in the media for commentary on Egypt and the plight of Copts, including regular radio interviews, print features, and television appearances. Tadros is one of the founding members of the Australian Coptic Movement Association.*

PART III

~

THE AUSTRALIAN COPTIC MOVEMENT AND THE FUTURE

23. FORGET SHADES OF GREY:
THE COPTIC SOLUTION IS BLACK AND WHITE

Anthony Hanna

Prior to writing this piece, I decided to search "Coptic Christians" using Google, despite having a hunch about what I would find. The search results generally consisted of the following: persecution of Coptic Christians and information on the Coptic Church, which focused on its persecution throughout history. That is it.

I then asked myself, is this our identify? Is this how the world views us? Are we just the "ancient Church" or Egypt's "Christian minority"—the "10 per cent"? Are we known for nothing else? Is this *the* Coptic identity?

Being a Copt goes beyond the word's religious connotations. Sure, Coptic Orthodox Christianity is a religion, and wherever one is born in the world we are all in essence Coptic, because we share a common faith and spirituality. But being a Copt is also an ethnic descriptor. The Copts are the direct descendants of the Pharaohs, and they gifted the world with the Coptic civilisation—a civilisation that has survived many invasions and rulerships under various dynasties and empires. The Copts are an ethnicity unto themselves and one that we should be proud of.

The unfolding events in Egypt hint that the nation may be on the brink of civil war. Although the liberals, libertarians, secularists,

Christians, and other religious and nonreligious minorities are fighting for freedom and true democracy, the Muslim Brotherhood and its supporters are intent on maintaining Egypt's continued demise. They are even willing to embrace violence and corruption to ensure Egypt's destruction.

We, as Copts, must act now. Ridding Egypt of a corrupt dictator (Hosni Mubarak) was only the first, and simpler, stage of the democratic experiment and the fight for freedom and social justice. Egyptians must now overcome their greatest challenge: removing the stigma of being an imprisoned people and learning how to think for themselves. Egyptians should be fearless and shape their own future.

The Australian Coptic Movement, through its affiliations and ongoing communications with domestic and international organisations, will join hands with all Egyptians and participate in this battle against oppression. The Australian Coptic Movement will help move Egypt forwards.

It has only been during the last 50 years or so that the Coptic Church has expanded beyond its traditional borders of Egypt and Sudan. A diaspora quickly emerged from mass emigration, at the height of Egypt's militant fundamentalism in the 1970s and 1980s. According to statistics on CopticWorld.org, a social media website connecting Copts around the world, Copts live in 52 countries and 709 cities worldwide. I never truly grasped our place in the world, until I watched highlights of the 2012 enthronement of His Holiness Pope Tawadros II of Alexandria. During this ceremony, Bishops of metropolitan dioceses prayed in German, Spanish, English, French, and Portuguese. And whenever I visit Coptic churches such as St Sidhom Bishay in Dural, Australia, or St Mary, St Bakhomios, and St Shenouda in Kirawee, Australia, I wonder at the Caucasian blue-eyed toddlers running up for communion. For a so-called ancient Church, we are advancing.

Many first-generation children born to Coptic migrants outside of Egypt (such as myself) believe that Copts are willing to lie down in the face of torment, all in the name of God. Many think that our only response to persecution and discrimination is to pray, fast, and, as they say, hope for the best. One of the greatest challenges as a member of the Australian Coptic Movement is to rally today's youth and raise awareness of Coptic persecution in Egypt. Undoubtedly, the youth know it exists and are aware of the atrocities that occur in Egypt. But because they never experienced it first hand, like their parents, they are less emotionally inclined to become involved. Although social media does play its part, the experiences are simply not the same.

Perhaps the following account will inspire the youth to action. It is taken from *On the State of Egypt* by the Egyptian journalist Alaa Al-Aswany:

> In the years leading up to the Egyptian Revolution of 1919, the British administration in Egypt attempted to break growing nationalistic sentiments in the country out of fear that a revolutionary movement would aim to seek Egyptian Independence. In the 1919 Paris Peace Conference, an ambitious Egyptian statesman by the name of Saad Zaghloul, led a small delegation to request that the international community recognize Egypt's independence and self-determination. To punish Zaghloul for his testament to expel the British, Zaghloul, who shortly after became Prime Minister, was sent into exile. The British Administration, aiming at creating sectarian divisions between Egypt's Muslim and Christian inhabitants as a distraction, appointed a Copt by the name of Youssef Wahba Pascha as the new Prime Minister. The move behind appointing a Copt was that the British believed Egyptian society will now be focused on internal fighting over nationalistic self-determination as a unified movement.

Aswany also describes the assassination attempt on the life of the new Prime Minister Youssef Wahba Pascha by Aryan Youssef, a young Coptic student. Youssef threw a bomb at the motorcade of the Prime Minister, which later earned him a hero status by all Egyptians. Now, although neither I nor the Coptic Orthodox Church would endorse the actions of Youssef, the events that unfolded in 1919 show that the Copts were just as politically motivated in calls for Egyptian unity as were many of the other political movements of the time. Since then, the Copts have been significant contributors to Egyptian nationalism and advancement.

In another book, *Egypt on the Brink*, Tarek Osman recounts the period from Egypt's cosmopolitan years of the 1940s and 1950s— when it held a position as a social, political, and cultural power in the Mediterranean and Middle East—to its eventual transition to today's backward society gripped by corruption, hard-line politico-religious influence, and rejection of social advancement. Osman also outlines the Copts' contribution during the early glorified years. He specifically mentions the Coptic families who advanced Egypt in areas such as politics, the arts, and economic reform. To witness Egypt's demise since the 1940s and 1950s, just watch an Egyptian film produced during these cosmopolitan years and then compare it to an Egyptian film churned out today. The regression is visual.

Since the first arrivals of Coptic migrants in Australia, we have seen the Copts implement significant contributions to Australian society on all fronts of the public sphere, using positive Coptic principles and culture in empowering the world around them, whether it be politically, socially, or artistically—or in business and community services. Some of these names many of us have probably never heard of, and we may not fully comprehend the influence they have made in their respective fields.

First and foremost is one Coptic Australian we hear of quite regularly: Nick Kaldas. Kaldas is currently the deputy commissioner of the NSW Police Force and his long and shining career with the Force includes assignments both domestically and internationally. The brother of Father Antonious Kaldas, Deputy Commissioner Nick Kaldas has naturally been empowered by teachings in the Church and the influences of Coptic culture. I remember some months ago when *The Sydney Morning Herald* ran a front-page story titled "Grudges drove surveillance, says officers", with Kaldas' face clearly on the front. The story outlines a secret investigation that involved implanting listening devices in the offices of certain police officers in an attempt to stamp out police corruption. One of the officers targeted was Kaldas, who was the head of the Homicide Unit at the time. When the details of the investigation unfolded, they found that the investigations were initiated out of envy—rather than identifying corrupt officers. The countless police officers, commentators, and journalists that came out in support of Kaldas was inspiring.

Our contribution to society does not stop there. Our experiences as Copts, in witnessing Egypt's atrocities against minorities, has inspired many of us to enter the political scene in the hope that what we have witnessed (and are currently witnessing) in Egypt never reaches the shorelines of Australia, the country we have adopted and grown to love. Individuals such as Magdy Mikhail (former Shire Councillor), Edmond Atalla (current long-serving Blacktown City Councillor), Maurice Hanna, OAM (current Mayor of Marrickville City Council), and Paul Sedrak (newly elected councillor for Rockdale City Council) have all made the decision that to bring about change, or preserve the values we admire most, we need to participate in the frameworks that can bring about these goals.

In Australian music, many of the younger, assimilated Coptic Australians may be aware of the rising talent within our community. Coptic Soldier, the stage name for Australian hip-hop artist Luke Girgis, has been performing in the underground music scene for many years now, drawing a niche following and performing in a range of concerts and tours around Australia and with some of Australia's largest hip hop acts, such as Chance Water, Bliss n Eso, 360, and many more. Girgis is also an avid supporter of the Coptic plight in Egypt discussing, in various public interviews over the years, the turmoil Copts face. Singer and Songwriter HR King, the stage name for Hany Malek, is another rising artist in the Australian music scene. Another up-and-coming talent is DJ Smokin Joe, also known as Joe Mekhael. As of the date of this publication, Mekhael is the world record holder for a marathon DJ set lasting seven consecutive days. Currently ranked twenty-eighth in the Australian DJ rankings, Mekhael demonstrated the values of his upbringing during the infamous cash scam involving school formals, in which he offered his services for free to students who lost large sums of money in an online DJ scam.

In business, there is the likes of the late Jim Selim. He raised a simple pharmaceutical company, Pan Pharmaceuticals, into an Australian conglomerate, and it became one of the largest manufacturers of herbal and vitamin products, with an approximate company value of A$300 million. The contributions of Selim and his wife, June Selim, to the Coptic Community, especially to Abu Sefein Coptic Orthodox Church in Rhodes, is praise worthy.

Yet there are still other notable members of the Australian Coptic community. Author, editor, and teacher Ramy Tadros (also the editor of this publication) has written a couple of interesting books, including *The War of the Words: Oppression, Egypt's Copts, and the State* and *The Writer's Manifesto: Rules for Writing with Class*. And boxer Sam Soliman, nicknamed "the King", is a former ISNA and WAKA boxing champion.

In the Coptic diaspora of the United States, where Coptic activism was born, Copts of the first and second generations have risen to prominence in varying social scenes, from famous restaurateurs and celebrity chefs to oil financiers, journalists, and social workers. An inspirational personal role model is Nermien Riad, founder and CEO of Coptic Orphans. This is the largest Coptic not-for-profit organisation in the world, and Riad has, through more than 20 years of work, serviced the needs of underprivileged men, woman, and children in Egypt.

I could easily go on, because although certain individuals may not be aware, we at The Australian Coptic Movement Association are knowledgeable of the good deeds performed by individuals. Individuals such as Jimmy Morcos from Melbourne, Australia, who has tirelessly offered pro bono and subsidised legal services for Coptic refugees facing direct harm. Brothers Michael and Andrew Guirgis are two boys I grew up. They started CAOS, a service focusing on enriching the lives of young African refugees in Western Sydney.

Whether we are tradesman, entrepreneurs, athletes, professionals, or aspiring artists, we as a Coptic community have the intelligence, skills, support, and potential to shape positively the society we live in. This, in turn, will see indirect benefits as the larger community recognises our achievements and contributions to society. Sure, protesting outside consulates at Martin Place in Sydney or Federation Square in Melbourne raises awareness in the short term. But long-term change lies in our ability to influence. And influence comes from our ability to achieve. We will achieve by dedicating ourselves to our passions and by supporting each other as a community. The Coptic identity is how we are identified as a community.

On a television show hosted live from Cairo during the ordination mass of Pope Tawadros II of Alexandria, the Canadian Immigration Minister Jason Kenney was interviewed by the Coptic television station CTV. Other than being stunned that the Canadian Immigration Minister found the time to attend the ordination when Egypt's own President Mohamed Morsi did not, I was pleased (but not surprised) with the praise that the Canadian Minister directed towards the Canadian Coptic Community for their contribution to Canadian Society and for their ability to assimilate with Canada's democratic and cultural values. The Minister also jokingly ended the interview by expressing his amazement at the number of Coptic Pharmacists.

I would like to think that we are a rationally minded people (most of the time). We possess intelligence, resources, community strength, and a willingness to give and volunteer. These are the ingredients that can position us to better the world around us—whether it is Egypt or our adopted country. We also have the power of numbers. As a community body, if we work together, nothing is impossible to achieve. The persecution of the Copts in Egypt and all the Christians in the Middle East can be overcome, if we cement ourselves in a position to implement positive influence on the world. Join political parties and lobby groups, succeed in small business and entrepreneurship, practise and promote your artistic talent, and—most importantly—embrace and work with each other. Dedicate yourselves, 100 per cent, to whatever it is you do.

We, as Copts, have experienced the demise and downfall of a nation dubbed "the mother of the world", and we do not want that mistake to happen in the countries we now call home. It is our duty, as citizens, to stand and fight against the injustices that we see occurring all the time.

Peter Tadros, along with many others, established the Australian Coptic Movement Association in response to the atrocities facing Egypt's Copts. It is a direct lobby and a human rights advocacy group. Coptic.

Coptic identity must be cemented in the environment around us so that we can present ourselves as a formidable movement, aiming to remove the shackles of society's ailments: persecution, discrimination, injustice, and religious fundamentalism. The Copts are promoters of democracy and freedom and the values that these themes entail. Our identity is defined by how we live our lives through Christ and how we promote these teachings in the everyday world we are a part of.

You, as an individual, can participate in our fight, and I encourage your participation for the sake of our rich history and to strengthen our community. The Australian Coptic Movement Association is not a political movement. We are a human rights advocacy *and* a community development organisation run by young volunteers that have dedicated so much of their time to looking out for this community. You can help by volunteering your time, making a donation, joining our members' base, or providing your expertise to our cause. By helping, you will become part of the Australian Coptic Movement Association—and you will become part of something much bigger.

~~~~~~

*Born in Australia to Coptic-Egyptian migrants, **Anthony Hanna** has been dedicated to fighting for the democratic cause in his parents' native Egypt. Holding a Bachelor of Commerce in Accounting and currently employed by a large, multinational, professional-services firm, Hanna seeks to use his management and corporate talent to empower Copts in Australia. He is working to tap their vast resources and end Coptic persecution and suffering in the backdrop of growing* *religious fundamentalism in Egypt. By doing so, Hanna believes that it is the Copts in the diaspora who will uphold their civic duty in protecting the borders of their adopted nation from such threats.*

A sitting board member of Coptic-based organisations, including the Australian Coptic Movement Association Ltd, Hanna also aims to help his community become invaluable contributors to Australian society.

24. SEEING IT FIRSTHAND

Ibrahim Messiha

Muslim or Christian? That is the question that lingers on everyone's mind. It is the painful reality facing many Coptic Christians living in Egypt.

Being treated as a second-class citizen solely because I am Christian is intolerable. Why is it that, because I am a Coptic Christian, I do not get to share the same power and authority that is given to any Muslim? This emotion is bottled inside, haunting many Coptic Christians today.

I completed my degree, like any other Egyptian, and started looking for employment; however, what happened next was my first real-life hardship of living as a Coptic Christian in a Muslim-dominated country. Many of my Coptic Christian friends have to experience the daunting task of trying to find employment with Muslim employers. They begin the interview by asking, "Are you Muslim or Christian?" thereby sealing their fate before they even begin and resulting in the painful experience of rejection.

In my case, I am reasonably lucky because my name is commonly given to Christian and Muslim men. So not many people suspected or even knew that I was a Christian. It was because of this that I was the first individual to attain employment, yet this did not last long. When the manager of the organisation invited me one afternoon to pray with him, and my immediate response was sorry but I am Christian, he immediately terminated my employment.

As a young Egyptian, particularly a young Coptic Christian, status or success was never foreseeable. Thus travelling abroad seemed like the only practical solution. After two long years of suffering and struggles, this lifelong dream finally became a reality. It was a long-sought ambition, after living in a country ruled by a dictator and encircled by ignorance and a lack of conscience—all shrouded by the cloak of religion.

Structure, rules, democracy, respect, principles, freedom, and equality are merely words I used to hear throughout the years of my schooling. However, not once did I see or experience what these words meant, or even what they looked like, in everyday life while living in Egypt.

Slowly, building the foundation of my new life in a new country, I was able to truly understand and feel what it meant to be respected, despite ones race, skin colour, or religion. I learnt what it meant to have a government run by structure and rules, as well as the importance of legal equality.

I keep on thinking about having all these rights to freedom in a country where I am not native born, and then I remember my native Egypt where I was denied these same rights. I ask myself, "Why would that happen?" And the only reasonable answer is, because I am a Christian.

Being given these powers and freedoms has had a profound impact on me, as I, an ordinary person, growing up with suffering and persecution in my own country, now feel happy and fortunate that at this stage of my life, I am able to enjoy these blessings, which I never could have imagined.

On the eve of the 7 January 2010, Coptic Christians were gunned down in front of their church in Nag Hammadi. *Why?* is the question many ask. The answer is simple: it is because they were Christian and they were practising their religion. Yet how can this continue to be a possible justification to end someone's life in this day and age? This day proved to be a turning point in my life. It affirmed the ideas that were firmly embedded in me growing up as a Coptic Christian: I would always be treated as a second-class citizen in my own hometown.

From this moment, I started to ask myself, "Is it fair that my Coptic brothers and sisters are treated as second-class citizens for the rest of their lives simply because they are Christian? Is it fair to leave Christians in this unbearable position just because they are a minority? Is it fair that I can have all these rights, whereas my Christian brothers and sisters cannot even find a job on the basis of their religious beliefs?" The only possible solution that I found was to employ these newly found Western rights and freedoms to conquer racism in Egypt. Since then, I have fought to support my brothers and sisters back in Egypt.

Not long after the Nag Hammadi massacre, I met with a group of enthusiastic young Coptic Christian Australians, known today as The Australian Coptic Movement Association (ACM). They shared the same views on the issues of discrimination and persecution. A few members even carried the responsibility of fighting for the rights of Egypt's Copts, even though these members were born and raised in another country. I joined the group and together, as one, we organised, planned, and implemented various rallies and activities condemning the Egyptian government and expressing our feelings towards the events that took place in Nag Hammadi. We scarcely knew one another; however, the only thing that brought us together was seeing each other's faces with that same pale look of sadness. And, of course, we were all fighting for the same common goal: legal equality and justice.

From the moment I joined the association, I can recall the feeling of gladness and relief that came over me, because I was sure that it was going to be an important day in my life. Our common goal was to defend any oppressed minority in the Middle East—and, in particular, the Coptic Christians. The purpose of the group is to raise worldwide awareness about what is happening in Egypt, from the persecution of minority groups to the harmful actions of the Egyptian authority and military and even the censorship in the Egyptian media.

No words can describe the feelings of those persecuted Coptic Christians who have had to flee Egypt in order to escape hardships and attain the basic human rights every individual is entitled to. Despite escaping from Egypt, the Coptic Christians have not left their burdens behind. They have not forgotten the continuous persecutions still taking place today. The persecution, which is becoming more evident each day, includes one man witnessing his own son's murder, another seeing his church being blown up, and another having his ears cut off for practising his religion. All these crimes happened simply because the victims were Christian.

Finally, I would like to extend my warm thanks to the ACM and, in particular, to Peter Tadros—the founder of ACM. Tadros has enabled me to shift my negative view of the events occurring in Egypt and turn them into constructive actions to help stop the persecution. He has taught me to redirect my defensive stance towards the issue and to employ a more proactive approach. It is important that we now try to systematically raise awareness of the truth and to expose what is happening in countries where the persecution of minorities continues to be a sad reality.

~~~~~~

*Born and raised in Upper Egypt, **Ibrahim Messiha** later completed his university studies before working as a site engineer. He then emigrated to Australia in 2007 to seek the pleasurable fruits of democracy, freedom of expression, and freedom of belief. Messiha is one of the directors of the Australian Coptic Movement Association and has been perceived as a strong voice for the voiceless. His life story and experiences provide credibility to his calls for change in Egypt.*

25. CONCLUSION

The Australian Coptic Movement Association

Do not turn your face away from the party. The Copts and Egypt need your support, thoughts, and prayers.

There can be no doubt that Egypt's Copts are facing a crisis. It is more than just a simple battle for "minority rights". World leaders conveniently talk of "minority rights" and "religious freedom" in countries like Egypt. Yet we are talking about a people who are not receiving the most basic of human rights—a people who are living under siege in their own countries.

Could the aggressive secularisation of Western nations be playing a role in the demise of Christian populations in the Middle Eastern and North Africa (MENA) regions? In the case of Iraq, we have seen the devastating impact of the Iraq wars, resulting in most of the indigenous Assyrian, Chaldanean, and Syriac people leaving their country. How could such a situation arise, and attacks against these vulnerable people occur, under the watch of coalition forces in Iraq following the toppling of Saddam Hussein by the West? The fact that such a minority could be subjected to persecution in the presence of Western armies is indeed mind boggling. The extreme secularisation of Western nations blended with political correctness has resulted in indifference towards the assaults on Christian minorities in Iraq and elsewhere in the Middle East and Africa.

Each country in this rather troublesome region has its own dynamics and complexities. However, there appears to be a theme developing across all Islamic-majority nations. What is this theme? Indigenous Christian minorities are not welcome; instead, they are discriminated against and persecuted.

The practice of "political correctness" and the aggressive secularisation of Western nations has resulted in countries that were once considered "Christian nations" to become indifferent to the suffering of their fellow human beings in the MENA region. Of course, secularism means different things in different nations and this can be demonstrated by a Google search of "secularism". Secularism also means different things to different people. To date, and despite demographic shifts as a result of immigration, the majority of Western nations still contain a majority-Christian population. But it is fair to say that even they remain apathetic to the persecution of their coreligionists in other parts of the world.

A blatant example of political correctness emerged at a meeting of EU foreign ministers in Brussels not long after the devastating Alexandria church bombing in 2011—a terrorist act that shattered Egypt and shocked many observers. In *The Telegraph* of 1 February 2011, Bruno Waterfield writes,

> A meeting of EU foreign ministers failed to agree on a condemnation of sectarian attacks over the Christmas period that targeted Christians in Egypt and Iraq.
>
> Talks ended angrily when Italy accused Lady Ashton, the EU's foreign minister, of "excessive" political correctness because she refused to name any specific religious group as a victim of attacks.
>
> Franco Frattini, the Italian foreign minister, demanded an EU response on the persecution of Christians after a New Year suicide bombing at a Coptic church in northern Egypt in which 23 people were killed.
>
> The Egyptian bombing followed attacks in Baghdad and fears, expressed by the Vatican, of persecution leading to a Christian exodus from the Middle East.
>
> Mr Frattini, backed by France, said it is pointless to issue statements defending religious tolerance without any references to the specific minority, Christians, that was under attack
>
> "This position is an excess of secularism, which is damaging the credibility of Europe," he said on Monday night. "The final text didn't include any mention of Christians, as if we were talking of something else, so I asked the text to be withdrawn."
>
> Diplomats have accused Lady Ashton of appeasing Muslim sensibilities to avoid a "clash of civilisations" after Egypt reacted furiously to a request from Pope Benedict XVI for better protection for the country's Christian minority.[78]

Political Correctness and the fear of offending others is one of the biggest challenges facing the Coptic rights movement. The issue is revisited every time a Coptic protest is organised, whether in Egypt or in the West. Slogans used at rallies are reviewed by community elders and paranoid members of the community to ensure that we do not offend individuals or Muslims. This can prove challenging especially in societies that pride themselves on free speech. It is difficult not to generalise when attacks against Coptic Christians in Egypt are committed by the Egyptian Government, police, military, sheikhs, Muslim Brotherhood leaders, and at times neighbours of Copts. To label all of the above as just "extremists" results in many slogans losing their meaning or the purpose of the protest being watered down significantly.

The term "extremist" is now used to describe anyone whose views do not conform to the norm. What is the norm these days? These are all difficult issues that many who work in this field have to grapple with. Ultimately, it does not matter whether the kidnapper was a Muslim, Jew, atheist, Mormon, or Hari Krishna. The fact is, people in Egypt are kidnapping young Coptic girls, and in Egypt's case they happen to be Muslim. This does not mean that all Egyptian Muslims are running around the streets trying to kidnap women. On the other hand, mere rumours of a Muslim women being assaulted or involved in a love affair with a Coptic Christian can result in mass riots and destruction. An example of this occurred in the village of al-Nawahid, Qena province, in November 2010. This is an excerpt from a Fox News report, "Muslims Torch Christian Homes in Southern Egypt", dated 16 November 2011:

> Muslims set fire overnight to at least 10 houses belonging to Coptic Christians in a village in southern Egypt over rumors that a Christian resident had an affair with a Muslim girl, security officials said Tuesday.
>
> The officials said security forces have sealed off the village of al-Nawahid, in Qena province some 290 miles south of Cairo, to prevent the violence from spreading to neighboring towns. They said several people were arrested.

---

[78] See "Baroness Ashton in political correctness row over word 'Christian'". This article was accessed on 1 June 2013 at
<http://www.telegraph.co.uk/news/worldnews/europe/eu/8296403/Baroness-Ashton-in-political-correctness-row-over-word-Christian.html>.

The attacks started after locals spotted a young Copt and a Muslim girl together at night inside the village cemetery, the officials said. They added that both were put under police custody as authorities investigate.

The officials spoke on condition of anonymity because they are not authorized to speak to the media.[79]

News reports such as the preceding tend to be reported as novelty news items, and they are rarely taken seriously by any human rights organisation or advocacy group (although in recent months we have seen various human rights organisations start to cover attacks on Copts).

The perpetrators are rarely reprimanded, and the victims are left to rebuild their lives from scratch. These attacks occur in the most impoverished regions of Egypt. Yet they deserve our attention, because we should be assisting those in need. These attacks occur regularly, devastating the lives of hundreds if not thousands of families every year.

Another reason for the general indifference to Coptic persecution could be that the issue has been successfully hidden by regimes in the region or that Western academics have simply decided to ignore it preferring to focus on more popular issues. Angela Shanahan wrote an article, "Fate of Copts ignored by the secular West", in *The Australian* during the early days of the 2011 Egyptian revolution. The timing of the article, which was written on 5 February 2011, suggests that this senior journalist was well aware of the plight of Egypt's Copts. The timing also hints that she hoped to expose the Copts' struggle during the pivotal point when Egypt was in the middle of a popular uprising, which was being watched by the entire world. Shanahan writes,

A disturbing feature of the crisis in Egypt this week has been the paucity of any discussion of the implications of the decline of the Mubarak regime and the possible rise of fanatical Islamists for the Christians of Egypt.

This applies particularly to the sizeable Coptic Christian population, estimated at 10 to 15 per cent of the Egyptian population.

The few vague references to the fate of the Christians were generally expressed, almost as an afterthought, regarding the repression of women.

This puzzling gap is indicative of the thought processes of many Western analysts geared to political explanations and impressions that have little to do with

---

[79] This article was accessed on 1 June 2013 at
<http://www.foxnews.com/world/2010/11/16/muslims-torch-christian-homes-southern-egypt/#ixzz2LioWgu9y>.

the deeper social and historical complexities of the Middle East, which in turn have everything to do with religion and the culture.

They really don't understand the importance of religion. Unless religion has an overt political face it is usually a mystery to most secular Western journalists.

Yet Christians have been out on the street with their fellow Egyptians this week, desperate that an Islamic outcome should be avoided.

Ignoring the fate of Coptic Christians is not new, and their persecution has intensified over the past 20 years. It is also a product of a general ignorance in the West about the broader history of the Middle East, where there have been Christians for 2000 years.[80]

The preferred way of describing the persecution of Coptic Christians in Egypt is to refer to it as "sectarian strife". This description has its origin in the Arabic language, with strife meaning *fitna*. And you will find that such terminology is used to minimise the extent of the persecution in Egypt.

Denial of oppression is another challenge facing the Copts. Egyptians are a proud and resilient people. They always like to boast about their country of origin. And why not? They have such a glorious past. Until roughly fives years ago, even Copts in the diaspora were in denial over the extent of the persecution. Some would say, "Yes, we have problems, but it is not as bad as you make it out to be." Speaking out against atrocities back home might be seen as an act of treason or disloyalty to their beloved country of origin. Fortunately, the advent of social media has changed the psyche of many unaffected Copts, and their offspring, living in the West. One is overwhelmed by the sheer volume of evidence of persecution that is readily available with a few online searches. Videos on YouTube showing victims of crime calling out for help and assistance are hard to ignore.

Yet the biggest denier of Coptic persecution is the Egyptian State, which is represented by its presidents, military rulers, and Islamist groups. No one realistically expects those responsible for the persecution of Egypt's Copts to confess to their crimes, which have been occurring since 1952.

Adel Iskandar is a media scholar and lecturer at Georgetown University. The *Egypt Independent* published one of his opinion columns on 6 January 2011, just days following a massacre of Coptic Christians

---

[80] For more details, see <http://www.theaustralian.com.au/opinion/fate-of-copts-ignored-by-the-secular-west/story-e6frg6zo-1226000017947>. This webpage was accessed on 1 June 2013.

outside the Two Saints' Church in Alexandria. Iskandar's article is titled "Coptic Exodus from Disneyland" and includes the following paragraphs in a rather satirical style:

> Just like Peter Pan and Cinderella, the Copts too have their own fairytale story in Disneyland. A story that has been embellished for maximum gratification, amusement and delusion. The fable of interfaith harmony where Coptic rights are respected, their civility acknowledged, their rituals tolerated, and their identities celebrated has stood its ground for many years and even has its own mascot. Like Disney's Mickey Mouse ears, the "crescent and the cross" has served as the logo of Coptic utopia, affirming the commitment of all members of Egyptian society, officials and citizens, to equality under the law. Any attempts to call to question this myth are barred completely.
>
> Last year at a conference at Durham University in the UK, I spoke about Copts and language. Following my presentation, an Egyptian colleague expressed his reservations about my discussion and argued there was no such thing as Copts. Since the term itself was Greek for "Egyptian," he asserted that as an Egyptian Muslim, he too was technically a Copt. Of course, he was both well-meaning and etymologically correct. Yet by forcing his assertion of the inseparability of Muslim and Christian in Egypt, he effectively erased the latter. His comment highlights a widespread naivety about an identity that has been in the making for over two thousand years. Denying the existence of a Coptic identity invalidates any case made by Egyptian Christians about predicaments they face due to their faith. One cannot make a case about something that doesn't exist. Donald Duck cannot sue someone for discriminating against talking birds.

Of course, the New Year's Day Alexandria church bombings caused shockwaves throughout Egypt and the world, as mainstream Western media outlets replayed the church bombing captured on closed-circuit television (CCTV) recordings. Yet if it were not for the dramatic CCTV records, the attack on the Copts in Alexandria would not have received as much media attention.

Thousands of Copts took to the streets all over Egypt, and clashes ensued at Alexandria and Cairo. Many observers credit these Coptic revolts as being the initial spark that ignited the Egyptian revolution.

The Copts in Egypt and the diaspora held a cautious optimism that the Egyptian revolution of 25 January 2011 would bring justice, freedom, and equality to all Egyptians—including Egypt's indigenous population.[81] But a few were also sceptical, because the Copts have

---

[81] The CIA estimate of the Christian population in Egypt is roughly eight million, as quoted throughout this book; however, recent statements by various Coptic Church figures indicate it could be as high as 13 million or even more.

been subjected to institutionalised discrimination and persecution ever since the previous revolution of 1952, and they have suffered tremendously during recent decades.

The previous regimes marginalised the Copts to the extent that hundreds of thousands of Coptic Christians were pushed out of Egypt to commence a new life free from hatred, discrimination, and persecution. During the last 61 years, the Copts of Egypt have endured mass massacres, mob violence, and the suspicious disappearance of their women. No one has ever been held accountable for attacks against Copts in modern history. Under the watchful eyes of Egypt's notorious State Security, Copts were massacred in almost every province and district of Egypt. Hundreds of Copts were killed and thousands were injured.

Coptic Christians participated in the revolution of 25 January 2011, and many Copts were indeed murdered and injured by Egyptian police during the Egyptian revolution. The Coptic community, in general, was encouraged by these events, especially the younger Copts, until the revolution was hijacked by Islamists.

The military launched attacks against ancient monasteries, and the subsequent destruction of the Church of the Saints in the village of Soul (Helwan Province) in March 2011 and the eviction of the Copts from this village just weeks prior to the Egyptian Revolution outraged many Copts and moderate- or liberal-minded Muslims. Coptic youth were massacred in the Mokattam Mountains, and in one case the ear of a Christian citizen was cut off under what appears to be a form of Islamic law implementation. Coptic protestors marched on the streets in large numbers to protest these events, and their peaceful rallies came under attack many times, with countless injuries and hospitalisations.

So what is the future of the Copts? And what is our role as Copts, coreligionists, and the international community?

The Copts are surrounded by Libya to the west, North Sudan to the south, and Hamas-controlled Gaza sits in-between Egypt and Israel to the east. Egypt's Copts are geographically isolated by nations who are not exactly known for their tolerance of Christians. Immigration is not an option for the millions of Egypt's Copts, except for the skilled and for the lucky few who manage to make their way out of Egypt to join millions of Copts in countries such as Canada, Australia, New Zealand, the United Kingdom, and the United States. Of course, many Copts in the West with a bird's eye of view of Egypt see no future for Copts in Egypt and are scrambling to get their families out of the country. To be honest, we cannot blame them. Is this the only solution to the Coptic question? Sadly, for many it seems like the only choice. It is not easy for us, who live comfortably in prosperous democracies in the West, to advise our family and friends back home to stay put and defend what remains of our Coptic and Egyptian heritage and faith. No doubt, there will be a steady stream of immigration to all parts of the world. But what will happen to the many millions who remain behind? What are the solutions? And what can be done to improve the situation for Copts specifically and Egypt generally?

Was the Egyptian revolution just one big party? A new form of reality television where millions around the world watched the events unfolding in Egypt from the safety of their homes? Where are all those who took to the capital cities of the world to stand in solidarity with Egypt?

We shall conclude with the following passage. It is taken from an article written for the Australian Coptic Movement Association by Suzy Hanna on the second anniversary of the Egyptian revolution (25 January 2013):

> The Copts were one group who had their strategy—join the ranks and call for the immediate demands of freedom, justice and equality, not just for them but for the entire population. They, along with their countrymen who sought the most basic of democratic values, have now witnessed a worrying rise in the attacks by extremists and fundamentalists on churches, Coptic businesses, the kidnappings and ransom of young men and women and the ongoing persecution of Christian converts.
>
> We do not ask for more than that the world looks again. Don't turn your face from the party that you demanded. Don't walk away from the situation that you encouraged. Watch as Egypt struggles to pick up the pieces of a broken nation, divided in terms of "Islamist and Revolutionary", "Man and Woman" and "Copt and Muslim".

Do not turn your face away from the party. Egypt and the Copts need your support.

~~~~~~

The Australian Coptic Movement Association Ltd (ACM) was founded in 2010 by experienced Coptic rights activists and a new generation of passionate young Copts and non-Copts from across Australia. The ACM is a community advocacy group that fights for human rights in Egypt by exposing the persecution suffered by Copts, advocating for greater political and civil liberties, and calling for the justice and security of Copts in order to promote democratic change.

By closely working with the wider Australian community, government bodies, the media, and other human rights organisations, ACM has quickly grown to become one of the most active Coptic organisations in Australia, accumulating nationwide support. This status is reflected and recorded in Hansard records and numerous national and international media reports.

The ACM has achieved many milestones, which has brought it to the forefront of the struggle for freedom. These achievements include organising rallies, lobbying the Australian government to pass motions in the Federal and NSW Houses of Parliament, conducting letter-writing campaigns, releasing media statements, providing support to Coptic asylum seekers, and encouraging Copts to assimilate into the wider community.

To support the ACM's cause, please visit <http://www.auscma.com>.

www.ingramcontent.com/pod-product-compliance
Lightning Source LLC
Chambersburg PA
CBHW072253270326
41930CB00010B/2364